The

KANYIKELA GENEALOGY

CONTENTS

The
KANYIKELA GENEALOGY

Dr. Cainan Ojwang

To order additional copies of this book, contact:
Xlibris
844-714-8691
www.Xlibris.com
Orders@Xlibris.com
837950

Tracing Kanyikela Community from the Luo roots

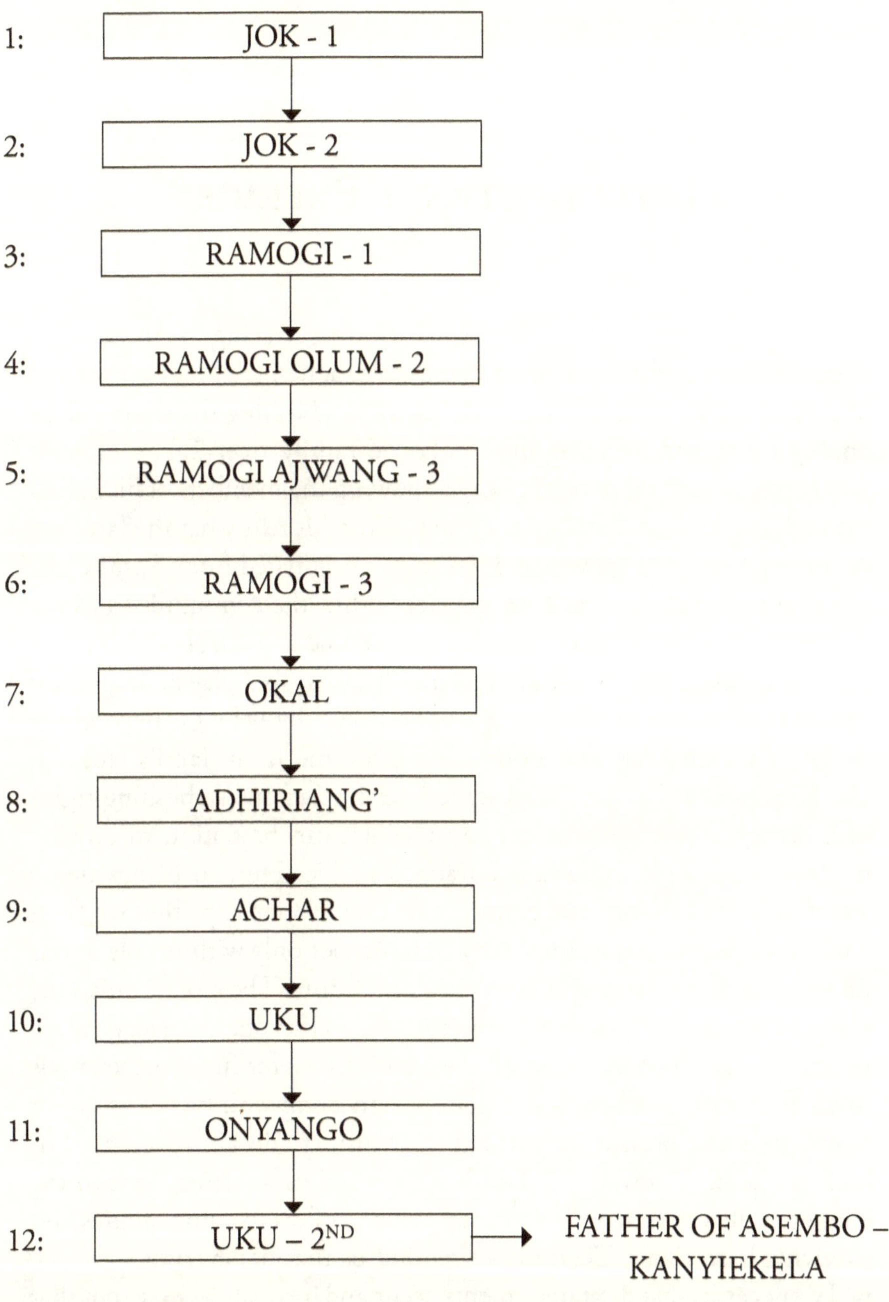

INTRODUCTION / PREFACE

Genealogy is the study of families including tracing their lineages, sketching their pedigrees relating to the collection of their names and that of their relatives, both living and deceased, establishing the relationships among them and building up a cohesive family tree. Taken literally, family tree is a record of one's lineage, showing the members of his family throughout the recent and even distant history. It tells what the family is all about, how it has grown, and where one originated from. Family tree can shape who we are, how we interact within the community and the things we value in our daily lives. It can help one to learn about his roots, cultural connections, ethnic identity and it can as well play an important role in helping one to discover where he rightfully belongs. Beyond the worth of establishing where our ancestors came from; family tree can also have practical value. It can sometimes impact on establishing rights of inheritance and rights to property, which can be critical to proving or disproving some important questions in life. Human beings desire attachment, belonging, and connection. The relationships that we form with other people can be incredibly durable, not only with people in our present, but also with people in our past and future. The more we discover about our past, the greater a connection we feel to our ancestors. As we record our own history, we open the opportunity for future generations to connect with us when we are gone. Connecting with members of our family past and present by learning their history fills an innate need in each one of us. Knowing our family history builds resilience. In learning about our ancestors' lives, we can see patterns of overcoming failures and surviving hard times. Their stories remind us that not everything in life will work easily, that disappointments occur and inequalities exist, but that we can recover, triumph, and find happiness despite hardships. Genealogy is a very important task for any family. It provides a way to connect with the past while building a future. It gives people a sense of where they came from, while also creating a sense of pride. In order to know who, you are, and where you fit into the world, you need to know where you came from. Family history also informs people about their health choices. Families that have a genetically heritable disease in their genes can encourage their younger generations to get tested for it. Stories about how relatives coped with a particular disease or condition can provide hope to those who have it. Family history holds important information about an individual's past and future life. It can be used as a diagnostic tool and help guide decisions about genetic testing for the patient and at-risk family members. If a family is affected by a disease, an accurate family history will be important to establish a pattern of transmission. A family history can identify potential health problems such as heart disease, diabetes, or cancer that an individual may be at increased risk for in the future. Early identification of increased risk may allow the individual and health professionals to take steps to reduce risk by implementing lifestyle changes, introducing medical interventions, and/or increasing disease surveillance.

This book is all about the genealogy of Joka Nyotieno family in Kanyikela community from the Luo Nyanza in Kenya. It is meant to teach the younger digital generation and those who cannot trace their family-tree from Kanyikela Community and particularly Kanyotieno family ancestral lineage. The details of the ancestors' lives are put into a meaningful landing that will be cherished from one generation to the other. The author has not distorted or altered any fact in order to make the reader comfortable or uncomfortable whatsoever. He used oral literature, oral interviews and historical records to obtain information regarding the kinship and origins of Kanyikela community and particularly that of the Kanyotieno family. The results are displayed in charts and written as narratives. Although the major emphasis is on Joka Nyotieno family following their request, other Kanyikela Clans and Sub-Clans have also been highlighted to conserve the truth on their settlement and co-existence with other neighboring communities. The book is a non fiction and the names mentioned herein are true and real for the said descendants. No tangible facts have been hidden. The flow charts have been used to easen the understanding of the reader.

ACKNOWLEDGEMENT

The idea of writing this book Came about when Ezekiel Ogola Ojwang invited all the Nyotieno family members at his home for a family reunion party. Many topics were discussed freely on that day but the one that caught peoples' attention was the fact that the younger generation members of this big family were scattered in diaspora and were not well acquainted with one another and this was seen as a serious problem. It also emerged that many sons and daughters of Kanyikela Community cannot trace their genealogy and therefore they cannot find their roots from their ancestors and know exactly where they came from and who are their kinfolks. A taskforce was formed and the author of this book, Dr. Cainan Ojwang was requested to spearhead the publication of a book revealing the Kanyikela genealogy and specifically that of the Kanyotieno family. The members of the taskforce included: The Patron of Kanyotieno family who is also a member of the Luo Council of Elders, Mr. Joram Lwambe Okola, the first Chief of Kanyikela Location who was also a member of Luo Council of Elders, Mr. Jack Francis Ojwang, the Ongaro Sub Location Clan Elder Mr. Peter Lwambe Okeno (Ombilo), the Kanyikela Ward MCA aspirant who also played a very important role of collecting, compiling and writing down the findings received from Kanyikela Elders, Mr. Milton Mathews Obote Orwe. Mr. Milton Obote was the secretary of the taskforce. The co-opted members of the taskforce were Shadrack Orwe Ongiro (Jamba) and Lameck Elijah Orwe. All the above-mentioned taskforce members did a commendable job. They sacrificed their time and energy to hold meetings to analyze the findings and to fine tune the manuscript making sure that all the narratives were accurate and worth publishing. This book project could not be complete without the enormous support and cooperation of the Kanyikela Community Elders such as Okeno Gudu, Isaya Okeno, Camlus Buga, Hezron Ochieng, Yustino Ogutu, Shadrack Orwe, Joram Lwambe Okola, Peter Elkana Agola, Wilson Ododa Oyaya, Caleb Obanda, Jack Francis Ojwang, Mahalone Ojwang Lwambe, Hanah Oluga Obambo, Okombo Otipa, Oyoyo Ochola, Obura Odongo, Eliakim Kasera, Menya Onditi, Tito Alal, Hesbon Odera, Shem Barack Odero and many others who were approached and were passionately willing to narrate what they knew about Kanyikela Clans and Sub-Clans. Dr. Cainan Ojwang came to be in close contact with the above Kanyikela Elders in 1982 when he was in High School and was given a task of collecting data for Oral Literature Project. The Project was about the Genealogy of Communities. Dr. Cainan Ojwang did the Kanyikela Community part in the Project. It was by coincidence that the Nyotieno family also requested him to do a similar job for them. It was not easy to get pictures of some old Kanyotieno family ancestors. Thanks to Madam Sabina Atieno Okola who struggled to get the pictures and made them available in time. To Ezekiel Ogola Ojwang who initiated the idea, members of the taskforce, all the Nyotieno family members and Kanyikela fraternity, I say thank you for your patience and willingness to read this book about your genealogy.

ABOUT THE BOOK

The search for family roots can be fascinating and interesting. Everyone's path is different, with its own peculiar twists and turns. Each bend in the trail, each landmark along the way, has its own charm and story. We only come to realize the true value of our family tree after circumstances have forced us to retrace our steps and learn the lesson they have to teach in life. This book is a genealogy study which traces Kanyikela Community and Ka Nyotieno family ancestry back to their Luo origin. Particular interest and attention were focused on the Kanyotieno family in Kanyikela Community, Luo Nyanza in Kenya. The Kanyotieno family met at Ezekiel Ogola Ojwang's home and requested for the publication of a book revealing their genealogy. The book takes into consideration and identifies some of the economic, social and political reasons that forced Kanyikela people besides other Luo Community to relocate from Southern Sudan through Uganda to Asembo in Central Nyanza to Ndhiwa, South Nyanza where they currently reside and having two Locations: South Kanyikela Location and North Kanyikela Location. It describes the events that occurred during their lifetimes that had an effect on their existence. The genealogical information of Kanyikela Community and particularly Kanyotieno family dating back to the 18[th]Century, was primarily gathered from oral literature and interviews with elderly Kanyikela people such as: Okeno Gudu, Isaya Okeno, Camlus Buga, Hezron Ochieng, Yustino Ogutu, Shadrack Orwe, Joram Lwambe Okola, Peter Elkana Agola, Wilson Ododa Oyaya, Caleb Obanda, Jack Francis Ojwang, Mahalone Ojwang

Lwambe, Hanah Oluga Obambo, Okombo Otipa, Oyoyo Ochola, Obura Odongo, Hesbon Odera, Shem Barack Odero and many other Kanyikela elders. The author had to compile and keep all these records, do the critical analysis with the help of the taskforce committe and come out with this book. The book opens the door for the readers to see the great wonders of the world in live pictures from sunrise to sunset. It tells a true story of every member of Kanyikela Community and Kanyotieno family from birth to death for a span of nearly seven generations. With this book in place, our children will never be left out for knowing where they came from. Since nowadays elderly people don't sit down with their grandchildren to tell them about their past real-life stories, this book will teach the younger generation to know their genealogy in a written form unlike in the past when our ancestors used to impart such valuable knowledge from generation to generation through word of mouth.

ABOUT THE AUTHOR

The author, Dr. Cainan Aol Ojwang is a permanent resident of the US. He was born and raised in Kanyotieno family, Kanyikela Community, Luo Nyanza in Kenya. He is married to Janet Ongati Ojwang and blessed with two children, Dammary Wendy Ojwang and Inan Ouma Ojwang. He holds Bachelor of Commerce (B. Com) and Master of Commerce (M. Com) of Jabalpur University, India and Doctor of Philosophy (PhD) in Business Administration of Maseno University, Kenya. He has 19 years' experience as a Lecturer of Business Administration at the School of Business and Economics, Department of Business Administration, Maseno University, Kenya. His book, "The Kanyikela Genealogy" talks about his own Community, Kanyikela and particularly Kanyotieno family where he comes from. His genealogy can be traced from top-down chronological order as from Ramogi to Kanyikela to Kowuor to Ka Okal to Ka Nyamudho to Ka Odwo to Ka Lwambe to Ka Wagany to Ka Nyotieno to Ka Nyowino to Ka Mahalone Ojwang to Ka Nyar Mosi (Min Apele) to his nuclear family of Ka Dr. Cainan Aol Ojwang.

THE LUO MIGRATION AND THE RAMOGI HILL SETTLEMENTS

All Luos came from Southern Sudan and settled at Ramogi hills in Central Nyanza so was the Kanyikela Community. Ramogi Ajwang led them to their first settlement area at Got Ramogi in Yimbo in the current Siaya County. At Ramogi Hills, they settled on the slopes facing Lake Victoria since they were good fishermen. In Central Nyanza, Kanyikela Community settled near their neighbours such as Kanyadoto before their further migration to South Nyanza, then known as Southern Kavirondo. They were slow and sure people but peaceful in nature. Some crossed over to North Mara and they were referred to as Joka Jok. Kanyikela inhabited the current Ndhiwa Sub-County area in Homa-Bay County in Kenya and others remained at Ndori, Ramba in Asembo Bay in the current Siaya County, Kenya.

THE GODS OF RAMOGI

Before setting off for the long migration journey, the Luo Communities were to visit great gods of Ramogi up the hills where only Traditional Community Magicians were allowed to visit for "fortune telling" to predict their journey ahead and settlement patterns. Being great friends with Kanyadoto neighbours in Central Nyanza, Kanyikela magician, Andang'o Ogutu and Odhiambo Rambo (Oracha) of Kanyadoto made the Ramogi uphill visit together. Ramogi Hill in Yimbo, Siaya County occupies a special place among the Luo Community. It is a revered place-considered the spot where the Luo people first settled during their migration from Uganda before occupying various parts of what is present day Luo Nyanza.

The Magic Stone

When the two community wise men visited the gods of Ramogi for divine interventions and consultations, Andang'o Ogutu, the Kanyikela magician was the first to cast the spell in order to be told what the future held for his community. He made the stone push and on settlement, the stone indicated that Kanyikela pattern of settlement position was South Kavirondo then and later South Nyanza. When Odhiambo Rambo's time came, he made the stone push and the stone settled where inwardly he was not happy with since he envied the Kanyikela community settlement position. However, Odhiambo Rambo did not tell Andang'o Ogutu, his Kanyikela friend about his uncomfortability but worked on a hidden plan to have his settlement position reviewed and changed by the Ramogi's great magician. Odhiambo Rambo deliberately and secretly left his shoes behind as they were going back home to enable him return to Ramogi's great magician for secret talks behind Andango Ogutu; the Kanyikela magician. As they were on their way, Odhiambo Rambo told Andango' Ogutu that he had forgotten his shoes and had to go back for them. Andang'o Ogutu triend to persuade him that they should reach home first and come back some other day later but Odhiambo Rambo insisted on going back just on that very day. Andang'o Ogutu finally gave up and made it home as Odhiambo Rambo returned to Ramogi shrines with an intention of sweet-talking the Ramogi's great magician to organize for him another stone pushing errand.

A Re-Stone Push Demand

On reaching the Ramogi shrines, Odhiambo Rambo sweet-talked the Ramogi great magician and explained to him that he wanted settlement next to his other friend, Bwai. Earlier on some communities had gone for the stone push and the first to make a stone push was Chwanya, son of Jok whose stone split into two, leaving a gap in between and this settlement pattern portrayed Kanyamwa-Kabuoch settlement on one side and Karungu-Kadem on the other side. Bwai whom Odhiambo Rambo wanted to live next to, made his stone push and his stone settled in between Chwanya's two split stones. This made Bwai to settle in the Central part of the Konyango brothers, Kanyamwa-Kabuoch on one side and Karungu-Kadem on the other side. Odhiambo Rambo as a friend of Bwai magician, Otuoma, wanted settlement next to him.

ODHIAMBO RAMBO SHORTCHANGES ANDANGO OGUTU

Odhiambo Rambo sweet-talked Andang'o Ogutu to do a second visit to the great Ramogi magician having convinced the Ramogi magician to give him a second chance for swapping the Kanyikela's settlement position with that of Kanyadoto. The Great Ramogi magician had advised him earlier on what to do to enable a second successful stone push exercise. Odhiambo Rambo visited Andang'o Ogutu with intention of fulfilling his own dreams. On this second stone push visit, Odhiambo Rambo was given the first chance to do the push and the stone rolled down knocking that of Bwai and settling next to it and this swapped the Kanyikela settlement fortune. Odhiambo Rambo therefore moved Kanyadoto people towards Kwabwai and this culminated to the current communities' settlement pattern.

KANYIKELA MIGRATION TO SOUTH NYANZA FROM CENTRAL NYANZA–ASEMBO

The migration of Kanyikela from Central Nyanza, currently Siaya County started in 1880s and the final settlement was in around 1903. They settled in the current Ndhiwa Sub County in Homa Bay County in Kenya. Like other Luos, they also moved together with other communities from Southern Sudan along the Nile through Uganda and briefly stayed in Central Nyanza around Rang'ala areas. However, as Kanyikela were planning to migrate to South Nyanza, some decided to move inwards to the Lake Islands, inside Lake Victoria like the Sirafung'o in Umadhi which were alleged to have better fishing grounds. Kanyikela people were great hunters and fishermen and they hesitated to move Southwards as they thought they were going to miss fishing. On coming back from these inward fishing expeditions, they found some of their people had moved alongside other communities such as the Kanyamwa people.

The First Kanyikela People To Leave Central Nyanza

Kanyamwa and Kwabwai were the first people to leave Central Nyanza to South Nyanza. The Kanyikela group which moved alongside Kanyamwa included the Kanyikela great warrior, Omach Ojango Kaluoch whose war tactics assisted Kanyamwa people to win their traditional wars with Kanyada and Kwabwai.

Kanyikela's Un-Coordinated Migrations

Since Kanyikela movement was not coordinated, some trekked with the Kanyamwa people, some remained in Asembo and others went further inwards as earlier said. These un-coordinated actions made Kanyikela settlement to be scattered inside other communities in South Nyanza. Those who remained by going to the islands in Umadhi settled between Uyoma and Asembo. However, a fierce fight erupted between Uyoma and Kalee and this made the Uyoma people to send away all their non-descendants and Jokanyikela herein had to flee back to Asembo.

Kanyikela Re-Visit to Ramogi Great Magician

The Kanyikela people who remained behind made another visit for fortune divine interventions for another settlement prediction. The intervention predicted that they should go and settle in Kamagambo-Rongo but by then the Luos feared the arrow fighting Kisii warriors. However, they came tracing their earlier brothers in South Nyanza and on their way, they kept settling amongst other communities which had come earlier as follows:

SETTLEMENT IN KARACHUONYO

Some Kanyikela people settled at Karachuonyo in Oriang' area and they are referred to as Jo Katuola while in Ndhiwa Sub-County, they are descendants of Joka Gori in Oridi Area under the current Chief of North Kanyikela, Mr. Elijah Abuto. They include among others, Joka Oyudho, Joka Ondiek Nyamasi, Joka Check Raguanda, Joka Onyango Neno, Joka Osinde Nyalande, Elly Weke Ogaja, Mzee Enos Ogwang, Dr. John Abuto, former Councilor of Kanyikela, Nyambero Onyango and many others.

SETTLEMENT IN KAMAGAMBO

Some Kanyikela people braved the arrow fighting Kisii warriors and went to settle at Kamagambo-Rongo like Joka Andango, Joka Owande, Joka Odiango Achoro, Joka Rabel Nyangau, Elly weke descendants such as Eugene and Karume who are also Jo Katuola and many others.

SETTLEMENT IN ORIDI AND KADEM

Another Kanyikela group which came later were Jo Konyolo where the first Kanyikela Sub-Chief, the late Akech Adongo came from. They settled alongside Jo Katuola or Jo Kagori at Oridi area. Some prominent members of this Clan include: Joka Alila, father to the former great South Nyanza Kenya National Union of Teachers (KNUT) Executive secretary General, Mr. Onyango Alila, Okongo Alila, Akech Alila, John Nyalele Alila, Joka Ouyu, Joka Ondiwa, Joka

John Akech, Father to Mwalimu Michael Akech, Joka Siling Obuya, Joka Ombuor, father to John Ombuor, Zachary Odiango Ombuor, Joka Menya Omango, father to Joash Ochieng Menya, Orua Menya, Samwel Genga Menya, Thomas Menya of USA, Joka Oluto, Joka Omolo Gari, father to Boaz Anyanga Omolo, Mwalimu Akech Omolo, Prof. Swao Omolo, Mwalimu Omango Omolo, Joka Adongo Wuon Oalo, father to Charles Arua Adongo, Joka Manason Oure, Joka Otulo Gumba, father to Achola Otulo, Omiti Otulo, Ojwando Otulo, Joka Maende, Joka Buong, father to Opete Buong, Camlus Buga Buong, also grandfather to John Buga, Cyprian Buga, Peter Buga, Otieno Buga, Joka Opete, father to Elder Abadho Opete, Joka Okoth Othuondo, Joka Nyuma Wuon Okonji and many others. Part of Jo Konyolo Clan moved past Ndhiwa because of fishing expeditions and settled in Kadem in the current Migori County at Got Kachola facing Lake Victoria. They include Joka Ombuor Okal, Joka Ndama, Joka Mbuda, Joka Obonyo, Joka Ladhri, Joka Auka, and many others.

KANYIKELA BEING THE MINORITY AND MARGINALIZED

This kind of scattered settlement made Kanyikela to be a minority and marginalized Community amongst other Clans which moved solidly as a block into South Nyanza, Kenya. The Kanyikela group that moved alongside Kanyamwa where the great warrior, Omach Ojango assisted Kanyamwa in their traditional fights made settlement foundation for the majority of Kanyikela Community in Ndhiwa Sub-County. With the second visit of Odhiambo Rambo, the Nyidoto magician, to the great Ramogi magician and his need to swap the Kanyikela settlement position and move towards Kwabwai, made him to leave a big forested land infested with tse-tse fly and this chunk of land was given out later on by the Paramount Luo Traditional Chief, Gor Mahia of Kanyamwa to the people of Kanyikela as a reward to the Kanyikela great warrior, Omach Ojango who assisted them to win their traditional war with Kanyada and Kwabwai. This portion of land, stretching from Rangenya, Unga and Otigo areas is currently occupied by the Kanyikela people such as Joka Odhiambo Oudho, Joka Hesbon Odera, Joka Awiti Boyi, Joka Sospeter Malago, Joka Onyango Andango, Joka Oinga Agola, Joka Japuonj Joel Orwa, Joka Lango Abuna, Joka Silfano Achola, father to the late Martin Ombewa Achola, Philemon Athe Achola, Dr. Cohath Jenge Achola, Joseph Odero Achola, Joka Onyango Liech Kilu gi ndawa, father to Prof. Jonathan Obel Onyango, Caleb Obanda Onyango, Moses Oloo Onyango, Sadia Onyango, Aduda Onyango, also grandfather to Kenneth Onyango, Solomon Onyango, Joka Achienga, father to Prof. Achienga, Joka Shem Barack Odero, Joka John Ober, father to Dan Ober, Elder Henry Ogidi and many others.

GOR MAHIA AND KANYIKELA LAND SETTLEMENTS

The post-independent Traditional Chiefs were also in many cases acting as Community Judges, Community Leaders and sometimes doubled up as soothsayers, Clan's medicine men and consultants. Gor Mahia was therefore the head of all Luo Traditional Chiefs (Paramount Chief) and he had the authority from the colonial government officials/administrators to settle communities and to dish out lands to other communities with finality.

LAND OFFERED AS A REWARD

As a reward to Kanyikela for their able assistance to the Kanyamwa people in their war with other Communities such as Kanyada and Kwabwai, Gor Mahia, the Paramount Chief offered Kanyikela land in Kanyamwa area left by Kanyadoto who abandoned Kanyamwa, swaped the Kanyikela position and moved closer to Kwabwai. He offered them this virgin forested land infested by tse-tse fly from Rangenya, Unga, Otigo Bridge on River Kuja connecting Kanyamwa and South Kabuoch to Pala market in Ndhiwa Sub-County. The majority of the homes therein are up to date the Kanyikela homes. These virgin forested lands were cleared with the assistance of South Nyanza District Commissioner (DC) who by then was called South Kavirondo DC. The DC summoned all the earlier Traditional Chiefs like Olima of Kanyamkago, Ongoro Afwata of Kabuoch, Pundo Agola of West Nyokal and Gor Mahia of Kanyamwa. The DC ordered them to bring and settle their people where the forest had been cleared to avoid re-afforestation but because tse-tse fly was causing sleeping sickness disease in humans and nagana in livestock, these Chiefs were reluctant to bring their people to settle here. The majority of the Chiefs silently declined the order and it was only West Nyokal Chief, Pundo Agola who moved one of his wives to settle at Unga hills to live with the Kanyikela people as obedience to the DC order and given this was his area of jurisdiction.

AKECH ADONGO GOES BACK TO ASEMBO, CENTRAL NYANZA TO BRING THE KANYIKELA PEOPLE WHO REMAINED BEHIND

Due to reluctance of other Community's Chiefs to settle their people in the cleared forests, Akech Adongo, the first Kanyikela Traditional Assistant Chief was forced by circumstances to go back to Central Nyanza to bring the Kanyikela people who remained behind when their counterparts were migrating earlier. Their coming was to help them settle and continue clearing forests to avoid re-afforestation.

BETRAYAL BY OCHOLA OUCHO

Despite Akech's noble idea of inviting his kinsmen to the new found land, Ochola Oucho (Wuod Nyodhil) who later took over Chiefdom from Akech Adongo betrayed him by alerting the Central Nyanza-Asembo Chief that there was one coming to take away residents under his jurisdiction. Akech was briefly held in Asembo for attempting to poach the Kanyikela people who had remained behind in Asembo. He was temporarily grilled and later released and allowed to go with those who were willing to move to South Nyanza with him. The Kanyikela People therefore took it upon themselves to occupy these dreaded lands and the government was also determined to rid the area of tse-tse flies. The lands were later discovered to be fertile since it bordered a permanent river-Kuja which was suitable for fishing, agriculture and livestock keeping.

Kanyikela Settlement Patterns

The first Kanyikela group who moved alongside Kanyamwa and Kanyadoto collectively settled at Mariwa Area in the present Kanyadoto Location in Ndhiwa Sub-County in Homa-Bay County. But later on, the Communities made up their minds to move out and explore further lands. Part of the Kanyamwa people moved Southwards towards Kadem (Thim Lich Oinga). Others moved Northwards in Kochieng', known as Kanyamwa Kologi while Kanyikela temporarily were left at Mariwa with Kanyadoto people. However, some unscrupulous Kanyadoto men raided Kanyikela homes when men went for hunting and raped Kanyikela women in around 1904. This incident made Kanyikela people to migrate to Osodo hills as others remained to stay with their Kanyadoto relative called Gumbo at Mariwa area. Some Kanyikela Clans moved to Thuon Gweno area and this annoyed the first Kanyadoto Chief, Ouko Obong', who organized and conspired with some Kanyamwa residents from Kosewe alongside Jo Kanyadoto to torch Kanyikela homes at Thuon Gweno area. Kanyadoto did not want Kanyikela to be free people but always wanted to stay with them and dominate them forever.

The Reprimand

Gor Mahia, the Paramount Traditional Chief and head of all South Kavirondo Chiefs reprimanded the Kanyamwa men for the heinous offence against the Kanyikela people for torching their homes at Thuon

Gweno area. These acts of animosity on Kanyikela from neighbouring communities made them to move further inland to Minya area. From Minya area, Kanyikela people moved further to other lands where they currently occupy in Ndhiwa Sub-County in Homa Bay County, Kenya such as:

RANGENYA AREA

The following Kanyikela people settled in Rangenya area and their homes are still there to date: Danda Oinga, father of the late Dr. Oinga Agolla, Ombwa Radolo, Ezra Osodo, father of Odhiambo Oudho, the Kanyikela Social and Progressive Union (KSPU) chairman, Nairobi Branch, Omach Kaluoch, Hesbon Odera, father to the first female PhD. holder from Kanyikela Community, Dr. Lona Odera Nyaoke, Awiti Boyi, Sospeter Malago, Onyango Andango, Mwalimu Joel Orwa, father to Engineer Moses Orwa, Lango Abuna, Shem Barack Odero, father to mwalimu Moses Odero and many others.

UNGA HILLS AREA

Those who settled at Unga hills included: Pastor Silfano Achola, father to the late Martin Ombewa and father in-law to Madam Meresa Ombewa, Philemon Athee, Dr. Cohath Jenge Achola, Joseph Odero Achola, Abott Magambo Achola, Mwalimu Dan Yongo Achola and Jalango Achola, Onyango Liech Kilu gi ndawa, father to Prof. Obel Onyango, Caleb Obanda, Moses Oloo Onyango, Sadia Onyango, Aduda Onyango, Isaya Obiero, John Ober, Pastor Daudi Achar, Isaac Onyango Ogunde and many others.

WIODIELO AREA

Those who settled at Wiodielo area included: Nathaniel Lwambe, father to the late Mr. Odete, former Principal, Homa Bay High School, and father-in-law to Mrs Rosemary Odete, former Principal, Ogande Girls High School, Ogidi Aroko, Menya Owuondo, father to the late Onditi Menya of Kenya Institute of Education (KIE), Oloo Agoyo, Otieno Mendwa, Abednego Orwa Odila, Nyawanda and many others.

MINYA AREA

Those who settled at Minya area included: Yustino Ogutu, Father to Kibera Ogutu and father-in-law to Madam Rose Kibera, Obago Ogutu, Onare Owiti, Onare Kwe, Dede Opoko, Joshua Otira, Mika Danda, Muga Lwany, Okebe of Kanyikela, Shem Owiti (Okew gi Yesu), Jakobo Kiluany, father to Mwalimu Opiyo Nyadek Kilwany, Obadha Gogi, Ochuodho Gogi, Opino Gogi, Osoo, father to Onyango Osoo and Rawago Osoo, Ongiri, father of Nani Ongiri, Adenyo Alaro, Gor Jonye, Rangudi Danda, Josaphat Adela, Aduda Manuar and many others.

NGUKU AREA

Those who settled at Nguku area included: Oyaya Kungu, father to the late Wilson Ododa Oyaya, father to Lukas Ododa, Omolo Ododa, Owiti Ododa, Josiah Obor Ododa, Odhul Ododa, Edward Onyando, father to Otieno Onyando, Moses Onyando, Mwalimu George Onyando, Sospeter Odiango, father to Jacton Odiango, Moses Odiango, Pastor John Odiango, Nyawuor Owino, father to Disco Nyawuor, Mahalone Nyawuor, Elisha Nyawuor, Okelo Nyawuor, Ogol Nyawuor, Charles Oricho Nyawuor, Okumu Owino, father to former Chief of Kanyikela South Location, Owino Okumu and many others.

WANJAWA AREA

Those who settled at Wanjawa area included: Okeno Gudu, father to Robert Oyuaya Okeno, Achieng Okeno, Okeyo Okeno, Japuonj Ouma Okeno, Hezron Ochieng, father to Japuonj Ernest Abuya Ochieng, the late Shem Odiero, former Chairman of KSPU Oridi Branch, the late Pastor Lwambe Nyauko Ochieng, Oguta Gudu, Odhiambo Gudu, Oyaya Obor, Okongo Obor, Joka Nyangoya, Joka Nyakongo, Nyaguda Ochondo and many others.

OTANGE AREA

Those who settled at Otange area included: Mathayo Orwe, father to Moses Orwe, Elijah Orwe, Daniel Orwe, Elisaphan Orwe Joram Okola, Mudkayo Aguom, Omolo Gari, father to Prof. Swao Omolo, Akech Omolo, Omango Omolo Boaz Anyanga, Eliakim Kasera, father to the late David Kasera, the first D.O. from Kanyikela Community, Tito Alal, the first Kanyikela Councilor, Moi Ondigo, Joka Misinjro, Joka Ongete, Joka Japuonj Nyambero, Joka Ogol Okwany, Joka Beto, Joka Sawayo, Joka Ondenge, Joka Mbwayo and many others.

RABACH HILLS (KOWUONDA AREA)

Those who settled at Kowuonda hills included: Obado Midheme, Magere Atang'a, Ongong'a Omuga of Kanyamimbi Clan, Onyango Ajoji, Fortenato Opiyo and many others.

THUON GWENO AREA

Those who settled at Thuon Gweno area included: Pastor Nicanor Agonda, father to Dr. Samwel Agonda, Ezekiel Ogola, father to Robert Ogola and father-in-law to Hon. Rose Ogola, former nominated MCA, Kanyikela ward, Gerson Radolo, father to the late Prof. Obura Radolo, Pastor Shem Amolo, father to Dr. Michael Amolo and father-in-law to Hon. Monica Amolo, Harison Aseno Nyangau, father to Onyango Aseno, Dick Aseno, Otieno Aseno, Okombo Otipa, father to Alaro Okombo, Omollo Otipa, Okech K'Oliech, Joka Ochore, Opinde Okongo, Oruko Kiasa, father to Eng. Antipers Oruko, Hon. Otieno Kiasa, father to

Hon. Jared Kiasa and MCA, Kanyikela ward, Pastor Cleopas Olang, grandfather to Mwalimu Ogutu Onyango and many others.

RANGENYA–UNGA HISTORICAL FACTS

Unga School was registered in 1958 under Kanyikela Sub-Location in West Nyokal Location. During this period, Unga was a Kanyikela Polling Station. Rangenya School land was donated by Ezra Osodo, father to Odhiambo Oudho, the Kanyikela Social and Progressive Union (KSPU Chairman, Nairobi Branch). Prior to 1966, Rangenya and Unga areas were in Kanyikela Sub-Location in West Nyokal Location. Rangenya and Unga areas had Kanyikela historical attachment since they served as the Kanyikela Community prayer sites. They also served as Kanyikela heritage and cultural points and former Clan meeting points. These were later annexed to the current Lower Kayambo Sub Location from Ndhiwa Primary School up to Unga Sub Location in Kanyamwa East Location and being administered in Ndhiwa Division instead of Nyarongi Division where the two Kanyikela Locations: North Kanyikela Location and South Kanyikela Location are being administered. Rangenya-Unga was the nerve of Kanyikela pre-colonial and historical activities. This area had Kanyikela pioneer leaders and had Kanyikela historical sites but has since been confiscated due to political reasons. The current lower Kayambo Sub-Location Assistant Chief Mr. Joseph Ambasa is a native of Kanyikela. The current Unga Sub-Location, Kanyamwa East Location Mr. Magambo Achola is also the son to Mwalimu Abott Magambo Achola, a native of Kanyikela Community.

KANYIKELA GENEALOGICAL LINKS

Kanyikela people are descendants of Uku the second (see diagram 1) who was their great grandfather. Uku was the son of Achar while Achar was son of Adhiriang'–remember Luos came from Southern

Sudan through Uganda along the Nile River hence such names as 'Adhiriang'. Adhiriang was son of Okal the first while Okal the first was son of Ramogi the third. Uku, our great grandfather had two wives: the first wife was called Dikiyo daughter of Yimbo Clan in Central Nyanza (Dikiyo Nyar Yimbo). Dikiyo gave birth to a son called Obola. Obola's wife was called Nyamimbi. Nyamibi's ofsprings constitute the Nyamimbi Clan whose descendants in Ndhiwa Sub-County can be traced to people such as: Aseno Nyangau, Okombo Otipa, Ochieng Milei, Hesbon Odera, Lango Abuna, Omollo Otipa, father to Ojala Multi, Owino Odhiambo, Odiyo Aluoch, Apiyo K'aluoch, and many others. Uku's second wife was called Wamlanda who gave birth to two sons: Onyango and Owuor. Onyango had four wives. The first wife was called Madindo, the second one was Otieno, the third one was Nyaponde and the fourth one was Gori/Katuola who was Nyaponde's sister. Owuor had one wife called Mikiro Nyar Seme.

THE MADINDO FAMILY

The largest population of Madindo family is found in Minyere and Achego, Gul Kopondo villages in South Kanyikela Location. Some of them reside at the foot of Nguku hills, Ariri Area and some of them live in Thuon Gweno village in North Kanyikela Location. The notable personalities of the Madindo family include: The Aduke's family such as: Ongete Aduke, Odero Aduke where the Kanyikela ODM Party Leader Johana Apiyo / Omusi Ongete comes from, the Oyugi's family including: Bishop Benson Opiyo of Roho Msanda Church, Daudi Onoka, former Kanyikela ward councilor, the Abuto's family, the Ndiga's and Opande's families in Gul Kopondo, the late Mwalimu Nyambero Muga, father to Benny & Jacinta Nyambero, Juma Jalang'o, the Ojwang's family including: Onyango Ojwang, father to Pastor Daudi Ogunda, the Ongoro's and Orimba's families, the Wariero's family including: Betow Wariero, father to Jery Mumi, Aboo Wariero, father to Pastor Aboo, the Shem Amollo's and Aboka's families including: Sammy Amolo, Hon. Monica Amollo, Dr. Michael Amollo,

Dick Okeyo Amolo, Javan Abuto, the assistant chief, of Kanyikela South, the Ogony's family where Joseph Agulo Ogony comes from and many others.

THE KOTIENO FAMILY

They are spread across both South Kanyikela and North Kanyikela Locations. The notable personalities of the Kotieno family are found in the following areas in Kanyikela:

Minyere:

Moi Ondigo's family, Shem Adede Ojako's family, The Akuta's family including: Boyi Akuta, Willseng Akuta, Onguko Akuta, Olewe Gengo and many others.

Nguku:

The Owino's family including: Okumu Owino, father to: former Chief of Kanyikela South, Meshack Owino Okumu, Orembe Abade, Mwalimu Mumbo Okumu, Joduar Okumu, Nyawuor Owino, father to: Mahalon Nyawuor, Disco Nyawuor, Elisha Nyawuor, Charles Oricho Nyawuor, Okello Nyawuor, Ogol Nyawuor and many others.

Minya:

The late Adela, Jakobo Kiluany, father to Mwalimu Opiyo Nyadek Kiluany, Nyaringa's family, Odina Ongo and many others.

THE NYAPONDE FAMILY

The notable personalities of the Nyaponde family are: the Muoma's family including: Obilo Muoma, Panaito Muoma, the late Senior Councillor, Tito Alal Muoma, father to: Joseph Ondenge-Jopa, Erick

Sonko, Adonijah Otieno Martin, Innocent (Kotewo), Joanes Owuor's family, the Rawago's family including: Oriang', Rwaka / Okuma Rawago at Achego Pap, Mzee Eliakim kasera's family including: The late D.O.-David Kasera, Onyango Agwambo Kasera, Hon. Silvance Wanjala Kasera, former Kanyikela ward MCA, the Okwany's family including: Mwalimu Ogol Okwany, Tom Ogol, Dalmas Ogutu Okwany and Broker Peter Okwany, the Origa's and Ondoro's families including: Mwalimu Isaya Ondoro, Agola Osano, Onyanja Osano, Sammy Auma Origa, Orara Ondoro, the Nyangoya's family including: Aiti Nyangoya, Opet Nyangoya, the Ondiek's family, the Ogaja's family, the warienga's family, Sawayo's familiy where businessmen, Lameck Ogonda, Leo Ondiek and many others come from.

The Gori/ Katuola Family

Gori was Nyaponde's sister who came to help her look after children and later got married to Onyango as youngest wife. They were the last to come during Kanyikela migration from Central Nyanza. Part of them settled in Oriang' area in Kendu-Bay and they are called Katuola Clan. In Ndhiwa Sub County, they encompass: the Oyudho's family including: Onyango Oyudho, father to former councilor of Kanyikela ward, Daniel Nyambero Onyango, Ogwang Oyudho, father to Churchil Ogwang, Abuto Oyudho, father to the chief of North Kanyikela Location, Mr. Elijah Abuto and his brother, Dr. John Obiero Abuto, Ndiga Oyudho, Pastor Amenya Oyudho, Martin Ochoo Oyudho, Amolo Oyudho, Alando Oyudho, Patroba Ogaja Oyudho, father to Elly Weke Ogaja, Moses Ogaja and Peter Ogaja, Ondiek Wembe's family, Ondiek Nyamasi, father to Gideon Owuor Ondiek and Charles Ondiek, Nyalande wuon Anjejo, father to Olima Nyalande, Check Raguanda, Onyago Neno, father to Elijah Oteko Onyango, Owino, father to Jabuya Owino, the Abade family, Mzee Enos Ogwang and many others. The above four Sub-Clans, such as: Madindo, Otieno, Nyaponde and Gori or Katuola make up the Konyango Clan in Kanyikela Community.

Konyango and Kowuor Hitorical Background

Owuor's wife was called Mikiro, daughter of Seme. She gave birth to four sons: The first one was Haya, the second was Misunga, the third was Bambla and the fourth one was Nyamudho. The four Sub-Clans: Haya, Misunga, Bambla and Nyamudho make up the Kowuor clan in Kanyikela. Owuor was a great hunter and black smith. One day while his brother, Onyango was away, a buffalo strayed within their homestead. He went into his brother, Onyango's house and picked his new spear and used it to lance the stray animal. In the process the spear got stuck into the animal's body and it ran with it into the thick forest.

Onyango's Wife Unhappy

Onyango's wife, Madindo was NOT pleased and when her husband came back, she immediately reported the matter to him and incited him to force Owuor, his brother, to go and look for the spear and bring it back. Owuor was very unhappy when his elder brother insisted that he must go into the forest to trace the animal and retrieve the spear. Though unhappy and bitter, Owuor followed the animal's footsteps into the thick forest and for many days he would climb up the tree branches to sleep as nights fell to avoid the marauding wild animals in the forest. Finally, the traumatizing search ended by Owuor spotting birds hovering and cycling above the sky, an indication of their prey nearby. The dead Buffalo had a spear protruding on its stomach to Owuor's great relief. Despite this, Owuor was terribly bitter on remembering that, his blood brother, through listening to his wife's voice had to force him to go deep inside the forest alone to look for the spear! Tired, hungry and angry he did not want to immediately go back to his brother. He climbed on top of a tree to see if there was a homestead nearby where he could seek for refuge. He saw some smoke from a far and climbed down to walk towards the direction of the smoke and later reached a homestead.

OWUOR LANDS INTO MOLA NYIDOTO'S HOMESTEAD

On reaching the homestead, Owuor met an Oldman and his sons enjoying the morning sunshine. As he approached the gate the men became alert and went for their weapons thinking that they were under attack by a stranger. After thorough interrogations, Owuor described and explained himself to the Oldman, who later calmed his sons down. He asked one of his wives to bring a calabash of porridge for the visitor. This homestead belonged to Mola Nyidoto. Owuor explained his ordeal and asked the men and their wives to take baskets and go with him to the forest for the meat but they were reluctant thinking that Owuor was setting them up on a trap. Noticing their doubtfulness and reluctance, Owuor suggested that the oldman's sons should leave their women to go with him to the site as the men keep watch and this they agreed. Owuor led the women to the carcass spot where they saw the dead Buffalo and each carried full capacity of meat. Owuor was heartily accepted as a good visitor. He stayed with Mola Nyidoto for a while as his brother, Onyango was worried that wild animals might have killed him.

OWUOR'S SURPRISE RETURN

One day Owuor decided to make his journey back to return the spear to his brother, Onyango. When his brother saw him, he was very happy to see him still alive. However, inwardly Owuor was unhappy making him not to disclose where he had been staying all along. Owuor one day sneaked back to Mola's homestead without telling his brother, Onyango. His friendship with Mola had grown tight and being a hunter and a blacksmith, Owuor would make spears and shields using wild animals' skins in exchange for food items which they would feed on as a family. This made their friendship to blossom and given that Owuor was staying alone in his dwelling house and would come back late from his escapades, Mola assigned one of his sister's-in-law to help in Owuor household duties and taking food to him. All this time, his brother, Onyango and his wives remained wondering where his brother, Owuor, would have gone to this time again!

OWUOR GETS MARRIED

As the girl kept doing her duties of helping Owuor, they got intimate and soon the girl became pregnant. The girl's name was Nyipir or Mikiro daughter of Seme (Mikiro Nyar Seme), Central Nyanza and was Mola Nyidoto's sister-in-law. When Mola Nyidoto's father-in-law heard of the happenings, he came to Mola's homestead to enquire about what he was hearing. Traditionally, when a man impregnated a woman out of wedlock, he was either to marry her or pay a penalty of a goat to the girl's father. Owuor requested Mola to convince the father-in-law to allow him marry the girl. Mola did as was requested by his friend and he was allowed to marry the girl. However, because those days, dowry was paid in terms of herds of cattle, there was doubt as to how Owuor would pay the dowry given that he did not have his own cows.

ONYANGO TRAILS HIS BROTHER, OWUOR

All this time Onyango was feeling guilty and restless over his brother's whereabouts. He was always a worried man over his brother's life status. One day Onyango met someone who had seen his brother, Owuor and leaked to him an information about where his brother was. Onyango traced Owuor upto Mola Nyidoto's homestead. He met Owuor's host, Mola Nyidoto and they talked at length and because Onyango was fond of his brother, he asked if he could also be hosted so as to go back and come along with his family to stay together with his brother. Mola agreed and Onyango went back and brought his wives to Mola Nyidoto's homestead.

OWUOR'S DESCENDANTS

Owuor's marriage was blessed with a boy who was named Okal, after Uku's great grandfather. Okal later married two wives. The first one was Ogiri daughter of Kaswanga Island (Ogiri Nyar Kaswanga). The second one was Anyolo daughter of Kamageta (Anyolo Nyar Kamageta). These two wives gave rise to Kowuor Clan. Uku the second gave rise to Kanyikela community of Onyango and Owuor descendants. They were collectively called Jo Kauku, (singular, Ja Kauku) later turned to Jo Kanyikela (singular, Ja Kanyikela) following the Owuor's marriage style narrated below:

OWUOR'S MARRIAGE STYLE CHANGES HIS NAME FROM JA KAUKU TO JA KANYIKELA

When Owuor developed intimate relationship with Mola's sister-in-law, Mola's father-in-law was furious and demanded a goat for a compensation for out of wedlock pregnancy. He was sure that Owuor had no livestock to pay as dowry. Mola's plea softened the heart of their father-in-law. But Owuor further pleaded that he be allowed to pay the dowry by installment arrangement. During this period, there were traditional wars where animals would be confiscated by stronger communities from weaker communities. However, great warriors could be rewarded by a cow or two as appreciation for saving the animals. Owuor was such a great warrior who assisted Nyidoto in such wars and in many situations, he would recover Nyidoto's animals and would be rewarded. As a blacksmith and a hunter, he would do barter trade and exchange his tools for animals as well. These he took along as dowry for the wife through Mola Nyidoto. The father-in-law would pay abrupt visits to Mola Nyidoto to find out the progress of the dowry payments. Nyidoto would then report that his friend was intermittently making payments, in dholuo it means "Kelo" occasionally further apart or "one after the other". This therefore made Mola's father-in-law jokingly say, that "Ero Osiep Mola kelo nyombo". Owuor was therefore mockingly referred to as "Nyikela", one who makes intermittent dowry payment in a scattered or sparsely sequence. Owuor therefore made the name to become "Ja kanyikela" instead of "Ja Asembo" or Ja Kauku. This name has stock with descendants of Uku the second thus: Obola, Onyango,

Owuor, Onyolo and Apiyo being consistently known as Jo kanyikela and this is a name we have cherished, adored and proud of to-date.

KOBOLA AND KAPIYO

Uku, our great grandfather had two wives: the first wife was called Dikiyo daughter of Yimbo Clan in Central Nyanza (Dikiyo Nyar Yimbo). Dikiyo gave birth to a son called Obola, giving rise to Nyamimbi Clan. There was one called Obiero who grew up in Obola's household and Obola even paid dowry for him to get married. His wife was called Apiyo. Apiyo was related to Nyamimbi, wife of Obola and here is where Obiero got Apiyo for marriage. They were later referred to as Kobola and Kapiyo because they both lived together at Obola's homestead. They grew on the side of Owuor and practiced same traditional customs with him. Obiero was given to assist Obola because Obola had no son to assist or help in domestic chores. Apiyo, Obiero's wife, was related to Nyamimbi, Obola's wife. This is where Obiero got Apiyo for marriage and why Obiero also comfortably moved to stay in Obola's family. Kapiyo' family comprises of two households: Kowiti and Kodhiambo.

KOWITI HOUSEHOLD

The notable personalities of the Kowiti household include: the Ogutu Yustino's family, the Obadha's family, the Onare's family, the Gogi's family, the Mikera's family, the Orima's family and many others.

KODHIAMBO HOUSEHOLD

The notable personalities of the Kodhiambo household include: the Opoko's family including: Dede Opoko, father to Javan K'adede, Ogwela Opoko, father to Pritt Atito, former Assistant Chief of North Kanyikela Sub-Location, Agak Opoko, Obado Opoko, the Andaro's family including: Kibira Andaro, father to Ongeto Kibira, Saoke Kibira, Owiti Kibira, Odhiambo Gombo, The Wadenya family including: Kapis Oyugi Wadenya, father to Mwalimu Aziz Oyugi, Omolo Oyugi, Okech wadenya, father to Mwamlimu Ali Okech, the Alaro family including: Owiti Alaro, father to Abungo Owiti, Akech Owiti, Odira Owiti, Adenyo Alaro, father to Angwen Adenyo, Abich Adenyo, Abungo Adenyo, the Oloo Athee family, the Okaka family including Owiti Okaka and many others.

THE KAPIYO-KANYAMUDHO HISTORICAL FACT

One of the Kapiyo sons, Yustino Ogutu tried becoming Kanyikela Assistant Chief. Joka Nyamudho alleged that Yustino Ogutu had taken a bribe of cattle to west Nyokal Chief then, Ondiek Ayieta, to favour his candidature. This allegation made Yustino Ogutu's candidature to flop terribly and because of this Jo Kapiyo felt betrayed by Jo Kanyamudho. However, one of their sons, Pritt Atito later became Assistant Chief of North Kanyikela, while his father, Ogwela Opoko was a prominent Sub-Clan member therein.

THE OWUOR ANCESTRAL LINEAGE

Owuor's wife was called Nyipir or Mikiro daughter of Seme (Mikiro Nyar Seme). Mikiro was Mola Nyidoto's sister-in-law. She gave birth to a son called Okal. Okal had two wives. The first one was Ogiri Nyar Kaswanga and the second one was Anyolo Nyar Kamageta. Ogiri Nyar Kaswanga had four sons: the first one was Haya, the second one was Misunga, the third one was Bambla and the fourth one was Nyamudho. Anyolo Nyar Kamageta had two sons: Odul and Achar. Joka Odul include people such as: Onyango Alila, Sila Ouyu, Opete Buong, Camlus Buga, Menya Omango, Adongo Akal, Okoth Othuondo, Maende and many others. Joka Achar comprise of people such as: Adongo Oalo, Otulo Gumba, Komba Mbosi, Manason Oure,

Omolo Gari, Ndama, Audo, Didacus Achola, Oguta Okelo, Ombuor Okal, Siling Obuya, John Akech, Were Akech, Oluto Oalo, Olimo Oalo, Anyanga Ogendo, Owuor Akech and many others. The families of Odul and Achar make up the Konyolo Clan.

THE KAHAYA SUB-CLAN

Haya was the first son of Okal and Okal's offsprings are from Owuor, their grandfather. This family is mostly found in North Kanyikela Location in Rangenya and Unga areas. The family comprises of prominent Kanyikela personalities such as: The Agola's family including: Dr. Oinga Agola, Muga Agola, Ouma Agola, Otieno Agola, Ateng wuon Oinga, the family of Osodo Harizon including: Osodo Nyangata, the Oudho family including: Robert Odhiambo Oudho, Obure Oudho, Dongo Oudho, the Owaka family including: Dr. Owaka and many others.

THE MISUNGA SUB-CLAN

Misunga was the second son of Owuor. This family comprises of prominent Kanyikela magicians including: Andang'o Ogutu who was Odhiambo Rambo (Nyidoto's) friend who went with him to the great gods or magicians of Ramogi hills as they were setting off from Central Nyanza. Misunga Sub-Clan had six households: Aduro, Nyachwiny, Omwoyo, Odero, Nyamangare and Airo.

ADURO HOUSEHOLD

This household includes: The Adhiga's family, Sospeter Malago, Caleb Biega and many others. Most of them are in Rangenya area while the Adhiga's families are at Ariri in South Kanyikela Location.

Nyachwiny Household

This household comprises of: The Odiwa family, the Achar Owande's family who are at Thuon Gweno area and many others.

Omwoyo Household

These are Kanyikela magicians including: Joka Osoo, Joka Andang'o Muga in Ondati area, Joka Dima and many others.

The Odero's Household

This household includes: the Mbwayo's family in Otange area including: Andang'o Samwel, father to Mwalimu Joseph Aenda, Odongo Mbwayo, father to Geoffrey Obura Odongo, Arua Mbuayo, Liech Mbwayo, father to John Liech and Pastor Liech in Thuon Gueno, Kiasa's family including: Hon. John Otieno Kiasa, Oruko Kiasa, father to Bon Oruko, Kenneth Oruko, Eng. Antipas Oruko, Agak Kiasa, Maranda Kiasa, father to Mwalimu Joshiah Ngaji Maranda, the Nyamwanda's family, the Nyakata's family and many others.

The Nyamangare's Household

This household comprises of: The Chiena's family, the Debe's family, the Awiti Boyi's family and many others. Some of these families are in Rangenya area while other descendants are in South Kanyikela Location in Ariri Village.

THE AIRO'S HOUSEHOLD

This family comprises of: Thomo son of Ojero, Ochieng father of Obudi and Onyango. Obudi was somehow abnormal and he disappeared mysteriously from his home. Nobody can tell where he disappeared to.

THE BAMBLA SUB-CLAN

They are found in different places in Kanyikela such as: Nguku Hills, Thwon Gweno area, Wanjawa and Wiodielo areas.

It has three households such as: Kakumu, Kodondo and Kokongo.

THE KAKUMU HOUSEHOLD

Comprises of: The Augo Oyoo's family, including Odongo Augo, the former Assistant Chief of Kanyikela South Sub-Location Mr Augo, the Oulo's family, the Orwa Onditi's family and many others.

THE KODONDO HOUSEHOLD

Includes the families of: Naaman Oringo, father to Ooko Oringo, Ephraim Lango Oringo, Fred Okeyo Oringo, Jekoniah Oringo, Abott Seda Oringo, Yongo Wuon Okayo, father to, Ongudi Yongo, Mwalimu Ongong'a Yongo and grandfather to Moses Ooko Ongong'a, the current Chief of South Kanyikela Location, Chiewo, father to Obogno Chiewo and grandfather to Mwalimu Michael Yongo Chiewo, Ogal, father to Ondiri Ogal and Lwambe Ogal, Nyalande, father to Rawago Nyalande and many others.

THE KOKONGO HOUSEHOLD

This family comprises of: Shem Nyanjwa, father to Ogwari Nyanjwa at Thwon Gweno area, Opinde Okongo, Menya Owuondo, father to Onditi Menya, Ogony Menya and grandfather to the current Olasi Sub-Location Assistant Chief Mr. James Omondi Ogony and many others.

THE NYAMUDHO SUB-CLAN

The Sub-Clan has three households: The Okech household, Odwo household and Radolo household. The Okech household include people such as Okech Koliech, Fotenato Opiyo, Onyango Ajoji, Abongo Nyachiala and many others.

THE ODWO HOUSEHOLD

This household comprises of: Joka Ndoya, Joka Odero and Joka Lwambe.

Joka Ndoya

Comprises of: The Onyango Waringa's family, Onyango Asamo, Erasto Nyawanda, Isaya Ochola Aboo and many others. It is in this family where the retired Senior Chief, Agolla Wawa also comes from.

Joka Odero

Prominent personalities in this household include: Eliazar Agoyo, father to the late Okebe / Assistant Chief and Kanyikela Patriort, Elkana Agola, Manaen Otieno, Oloo Agoyo, Pastor Cleopas Olang, father to Mudkayo Olang, Simeon Onyango, and grandfather to Mwalimu Meshack Ogutu Onyango and Mwalimu Nicanor Agonda Onyango, Shem Barack Odero, father to Mwalimu Moses Odero, Onyango Ogunde's family, Prof. Jonathan Obel Onyango, Bishop Caleb Obanda,

Mwalimu Richard Wandugu Anyango, Obuya Lwambe, Wilson Palo and many others. Mwalimu Zedekiah Odhiambo and Madam Lensa Odhiambo also come from this family.

Joka Lwambe

There are five households in this family: Okuon, Asigo, Ogidi, Onyango and Wagany.

THE OKUON'S HOUSEHOLD

Comprises of the descendants of Atwenga, the first wife of Nyamudho. It includes the families of: Odhiambo, father of Omuto Nyandera, Okwach son of Odhiambo and grandfather to Jayalo son of Okwach, Mr. Bush Justus, Alphonce Omuto who stays in Homa-Bay, Sila Onyango, father to Okinyi Sila and Dan (Tayo), Achidi, father to Elder Jackson Achidi and many others.

THE ASIGO HOUSEHOLD

The second wife of Nyamudho was Akal. She gave rise to: Asigo, Ogidi and Onyango.

The notable personalities of the Asigo household include: Odero, father of Osongo, the Dula's families including: Odero Dula, Ombok Dula, father to Mwalimu Martin Ombok, Timotheo Etah, father to Mwalimu Fredrick Ojwang (Majiwa), Mwalimu Zedy Etah, Naftali Radolo, father to Orwe Akira, Achieng'a, father to George Odero and Prof. Ogembo Achieng'a, Otieno Masadha, father to Johnson Odero Otieno (A person), Mrs. Silpa Nyagilo, Nahason Agwom, father to Hezekiah Agwom, Jason Polo, chair of Kalwambe family and many others.

THE OGIDI HOUSEHOLD

The Ogidi household had three Sub-househols: Oyaya, Athee and Odero.

Joka Oyaya

Prominent Personalities include: Ododa Oyaya, father to Lukas Ododa, Omollo Ododa, Oyaya Ododa, Nelson Ododa, Odhul Ododa, Obor Ododa, Mwalimu Owiti Ododa, Sospeter Odiango Oyaya father to Jactone Odiango, Moses Odiango, Pastor John Odiango, Kennedy Odiango, Martin Odiango, Edward Onyando Oyaya, father to Otieno Onyando Moses Onyando, Mwalimu George Onyando, Josiah Obor Oyaya, father to Jonah Obor, Oyaya Obor, Okongo Obor, Omiya Oyaya, Oluoch Oyaya, Okungu Owiti, father to Owiti Okungu and Elly Odeny Okungu. and many others. Here we also have the current Assistant Chief of Ongaro Sub-Location, Maurice Odhiambo, son of Ododa Oyaya, who was also the Assistant Chief of Kanyikela Sub-Location from the year 1951-1954.

Joka Athee

Prominent Personalities include: Pastor Silfano Achola, father to Martin Ombewa, former AEO from Kanyikela and father in-law to Madam Meresa Ombewa, Philemon Athee Achola, Dr. Cohath Jenge Achola, Joseph Odero Achola, Abott Magambo Achola, Mwalimu Dan Yongo Achola and Jalango Achola, Benjamin Anguk, father to Tukiko Anguk and Elder Caleb Anguk, here we also have the Assistant Chief, Nick Abott Acholla of Unga Sub Location in East Kanyamwa Location.

Joka Odero

Prominent Personalities include: Pastor Daudi Achar, Absalom Okello, Isaya Aboo, Isaya Obiero, Joel Orwa, Barnabas Okeyo, Nathaniel Lwambe, Elder Henry Ogidi, Mwalimu Obadia Achar,

Eng. Moses Orwa, Willis Odette, Mwalimu Okinyi Orwa and many others. Here we also have Mwalimu Odete Lwambe, former Homa Bay High School principal and Mrs. Rosemary Odete, former Principal of Ogande Girls High School. They are majorly found at the foot of Unga Hills and Wiodielo areas.

Joka Onyango

This group comprises families including: Hezron Ochieng', father to Mwalimu Ernest Abuya Ochieng, Akal Ochieng, the late Pastor Lwambe Ochieng (Nyauko), the late Kanyikela Patriot, Shem Onyango Ochieng (Odiero) and grandfather to Sony Lwambe, Nyakong'o Omuga, father to Oyugi Nyakongo and grandfather to Vincent Okinyi Oyugi, Kapis Nyaguda, father to Yambo Nyaguda, Aran Ombok, Richard Onyango (The dentist), Odhuno Josaphat, Samwel Opapa Muga, Agola Palo and many others.

Joka Radolo

This group comprises: Jo Kagutu and Jo Kotuona. They live at Thuon Gweno and Wiodielo areas.

Jo Kagutu

This group includes: The Abuya family including: Ongudi Abuya in Migori, Okelo Obama, father to Okongo Okelo and grandfather to Oweru Okongo, Abiero, father to Ezekiel Ogola Abiero, Dan Odoyo Abiero, Samson Abiero and grandfather to Robert Ogola, Ogola Ogola, Omolo Ogola and father-in-law to Hon. Rose Otieno, former nominated MCA of Kanyikela ward, Eliakim Obambo, father to James Obambo, Ogola Obambo, Aindo Obambo, Elijah Obambo, Mzee Ochore, father to Abony Ochore and grandfather to Amala Abony, Pastor Nicanor Agonda Radolo, father to Dr. Samwel Agonda, Ojijo Agonda, Gerson Radolo, father to Prof. Obura Radolo (Kariuki), Otieno Radolo, Ezekiel Ogola Radolo (Bobby), Fibi Ododa Okach, Zadock Owino, Joseph

Omolo, Wilson Okach, Zablon Okach, father to Ogola Okach (Pajero) and many others.

Jo Kotuona

This group comprises: The late Seko Okach, Mzee Joel Odwo, father to Narkisho Ombewa (Jarateng), Otieno Odwo, Timon Odwo and grandfather to Wyclifee Odeny Ombewa and Timon Otieno, the Lwany's family including: Ogwati Lwany, Ogalo Lwany, Magolo Lwany, Muga Lwany, Elijah Lwany and Odinga Lwany.

Joka Wagany

Nyamudho's third wife was called Chicho who gave rise to: Joka Nyodhil, Joka Nyandhe and Joka Nyotieno. The above three Sub-Clans make up Joka Wagany.

Joka Nyodhil

Comprises of the Ochola Oucho (Oroki) family. Ochola Oroki had six wives after donating one, Ooro Nyar Nyambok to Gudu Nyaruath. The first one was Odalo mother of Gor. The second one was Yaga daughter of Opiyo (Yaga Nyar Opiyo). Yaga had two sons namely: Nyasoro Ochola and Ojwang Ochola. The third one was Atieno Nyalego who had two sons namely: Oyoyo Ochola and Carey Francis Ochola (Karanga). The fourth one was Abila Nyotieno, who had two sons as well namely: Ongoro Ochola and Aduol Ochola. The fifth one was Marando Nyotieno, who had a son called Otieno Ochola. The sixth and the last one was Oboko daughter of Kachieng', who had a son called Akowa Ochola. The above Kochola family constitute Joka Nyodhil. The notable Personalities in this family include: The late Dr. Michael Ombwa Nyasoso who died and buried in Migori County, Kazango Philip, Moses Koigi, Mrs. Botty Nyagwasi, Mwalimu Evince Otieno, Kwaru Ocholla Ongoro, Sammy Aduol and many others.

Historical Facts:

When the first Kanyikela Assistant-Chief, Akech went to bring Jo Kanyikela who remained behind in Central Nyanza, Asembo, Ochola Oucho, the grandfather of these descendants wrote a letter to the colonial administration based in Kisumu that Akech was going to poach the residents of Asembo to South Nyanza. Akech was briefly held in Asembo but later released and came back with those who were willing to come with him to South Nyanza. Ochola Oucho was the third Kanyikela Assistant Chief after Akech between 1928-1933. Akech died in 1938.

Joka Nyandhe

The mother in this household was known as Matu, daughter of Ndhe (Matu Nyandhe). The household is therefore known as "Nyandhe" household for, daughter of "Ndhe". Matu Nyandhe had three sons: Otieno, Gudu and Ongiro.

Joka Otieno

Comprises of: Samson Wagany, father to Otieno Wagany, Peter Wagany, Musa Wagany (Ongo wange riek), Domnick Chondo Wagany, Silfano Achola Wagany (Asilo), Joshua Ongeng, father to Asulo (Wendo oke galot), Simeon Ongeng, and grandfather to Moses Simeon Ongeng, Onyango Asulo, Lucky Obengle, Johnson Ongoro Asulo, Joshua Otieno, father to, Gudu Otieno and Felix Ooro Otieno, Adhiambo Pene and many others.

Joka Gudu

This household had: Okeno Gudu, father to Robert Oywaya Okeno, George Ouma Okeno, Joseph Kasera Okeno, Achieng Okeno (Baa), Okeyo Calvins, Ajuoga Okeno, Nyandera Okeno, Dinah Okeno, Ongeng Okeno, Wagany Gudu who died in Tanzania and his clothes were buried in Wanjawa area near to Okeno Gudu's homestead, Odhiambo Gudu, father to Joshiah Odhiambo and Ochola Odhiambo, Oguta Gudu, father to Haggai Oguta and many others.

Joka Ongiro

Comprises of: Dominicus Wagany Ongiro, Shadrack Orwe Ongiro (YBL), Johana Okeno Ongiro, Josiah Obor Ongiro and many others. Prominent descendants of this family are: Mzee Shadrack Orwe Ongiro (YBL), Paul Wagany, Awall K'ongiro son of Shadrack Orwe (Jamba), Chodi Obor, Mr. Otibe, Orede Fredrick (Ja Pii) and many others.

Joka Nyotieno

Oluga Nyotieno was the wife of Oyaya, the father of both Elijah Lwambe and Mathayo Orwe. Oyaya had two wives who were sisters. The first one was Hanah Olugah Nyotieno and the second one was Flora Weke Nyotieno. Both the wives of Oyaya were daughters of Otieno from Uyoma hence, "NYOTIENO". Oyaya was a Chief in Central Nyanza (Asembo) during the pre-independence period. He died in Central Nyanza so was the first wife, Hanah Oluga leaving behind the second wife, Weke, who was now taking care of the Oyaya's children, Mathayo Orwe and Elijah Lwambe. Weke, the second wife of Oyaya was inherited by Gudu from Nyandhe's family, when Kanyikela people were still living in Central Nyanza, Asembo. Elijah Lwambe was Oyaya's eldest son and he travelled far to work for Railways Company in Nairobi. He was converted to Church Missionary Society (CMS), now Anglican Church of Kenya (ACK). Since CMS was the Crown Church and all civil servants were encouraged to be church members, Elijah Lwanbe being a civil servant was converted into this faith. Gudu and Weke's Group travelled to South Gnyanza in the current Ndhiwa Sub-County and stayed at Thuon Gweno area under Ombwa Radolo's homestead. Ombwa Radolo was from Nyodhil's household. Since Nyodhil's son, Ochola Oucho had seven wives and Gudu had none (he only had Weke Nyotieno whom he inherited after Oyaya's death but in Luo culture an inherited woman is not counted as a legal wife), Ochola Oucho gave Gudu his own wife by the name Ooro daughter of Nyambok (Ooro Nyar Nyambok). Gudu and Ooro Nyar Nyambok had four sons: Okeno Gudu, Odhiambo Gudu, Oguta Gudu and Wagany Gudu. It is at Thuon Gweno where Orwe married Dina Achienge as his first wife in 1911. Orwe was being taken care of by Gudu and Weke. From Thwon Gweno area they moved to Minya area before finally moving to Otange area.

Orwe's Marriage to Dina Achienge

Gudu was Gor Mahia's magician and they had known each other when they were still in Central Nyanza. Gor Mahia was the Paramount Chief among all the Luo Chiefs (Only the Luo Heroes were appointed as Chiefs). Dina's father, Ochuodho was one of Gor Mahia's wise men and advisors. Orwe "Angwani", as he was popularly known was a porter trader who was moving goods to and from Kisii town in Kenya. He was the son of Oyaya, the former Chief of Asembo. Since his father was the Chief of Asembo and Ochuodho, Dina's father was also one of the advisors of Gor Mahia, the Paramount Chief, it was easy for Orwe to get married to Dina as per the earlier Luo cultural chiefdom marital practices.

From Thuon Gweno to Minya

Those who moved from Thuon Gweno to Minya with Gudu included: Orwe and his wife, Dina, Ooro Nyar Nyambok, wife of Gudu, Okeno, wife of Wagany and Ong'iro, who at this time inherited Weke Nyotieno (Oticha), mother of both Elijah Lwambe and Mathayo Orwe.

FROM MINYA TO OTANGE

From Minya the above-named people moved to Otange area. Elijah Lwambe came back from Nairobi and joined his brother, Orwe at Otange under Ong'iro, who inherited their mother, Weke Nyotieno. Being the eldest son, Lwambe put up a home at Otange where he stayed with his younger brother, Orwe. Each later made their different homesteads. Lwambe's wife was called Rael Ndiawo (Nyowino). From Otange they moved to Nguku-Majengo Area and with the coming of white men who brought the Seventh Day Adventist Church (SDA) at Rapedhi in 1911, Orwe briefly stayed at Rapedhi and got converted to SDA. Orwe's second wife, Rusalia Nyapara, mother of Elijah Orwe died and was buried at Rapedhi during this period.

SDA CHURCH RAPEDHI

Kanyikela elders who donated Rapedhi SDA Church land were: Cleopas Olang, Eliazar Agoyo and Barnabas Okeyo. All this time Elijah Lwambe and Mathayo Orwe's mother, Weke, was still inherited by Ong'iro, who moved with them to Minya and then to Otange. From Rapendhi, Orwe came along with James Orwe and Elijah Dande, father to Joshua Ogola Dande, as Church teachers who helped him to start a Church and School at Otange. Due to some personal reasons, Orwe and Lwambe separated and settled at different places. Lwambe moved to Nguku-Majengo area and later to Oridi where he started CMS Church and School while Orwe moved to Otange, where he brought SDA Church and School in 1920.

ORWE ARRESTED BY ASSISTANT CHIEF, AKECH ADONGO

Akech Adongo, the first Assistant Chief of Kanyikela was friendly to Orwe's elder brother, Elijah Lwambe. Lwambe was his interpreter during the arrival of the Europeans. However, Akech arrested Orwe, Lwambe's brother and took him to a cell in Kisii having charged him with felony. Mathayo Orwe died in 1930 while his brother Lwambe died later at Oridi in 1939. This was after his friend Akech, the first Kanyikela Assistant Chief had died a year earlier in 1938. Rael Ndiawo Nyowino, the wife of Elijah Lwambe was thereafter inherited by Dula wuon Ombok and later by Hezron Ochieng, the father to Mwalimu Ernest Abuya Ochieng.

HISTORICAL FACTS:

Oyaya, father of Mathayo Orwe and Elijah Lwambe was the Chief in Central Nyanza, Asembo but was betrayed by Oyaya, father of Ododa from Kogidi Sub-Clan, who later took over his position as the Chief of Asembo. Likewise, Akech, the first Assistant Chief of Kanyikela, was also betrayed by Ochola Oucho who later on took over his administrative position.

ELDERS WHO ACCOMPANIED MATHAYO ORWE TO OTANGE

Mathayo Orwe and his wife, Dina Achienge went to Otange where he built his home and started Otange SDA Church and school. Mzee Ongiro who inherited his mother, Flora Weke, went with him to stand in as his father at the home building site. The Kanyikela elders who accompanied him were: Ogidi Jabwana, James Orwe, Isaya Obiero, Josiah Obor, Daudi Omolo Okumu and some new SDA converts from Rapedhi Mission such as: Joshua Liech Ondenge, Daudi Opanga, Mika Awino, Joel Andango and many others. He later on married Damar Aloo Nyowiti and since he was now a polygamist, he couldn't take part in the church leadership as required by the doctrines of the SDA Church. Some evangelists such as Elijah Dande, Elkana Nyariwo, Zephaniah Ouko and Fanuel Nguka were sent from Rapedhi Mission to take over the Church leadership. Orwe was enthusiastic about development projects. Elijah Lwambe, his eldest brother, who was working in Nairobi for the Railways company, would send an assortment of wares such as clothing materials and others which Orwe would sell to people in Kadem and even Tanganyika and the proceeds he would use to buy cows, sheep and goats which made the Nyotieno family to prosper in Otange area.

Orwe met his sudden death in 1930 when he was gored by a raging wild beast which was being chased by a group of hunters towards Oyombe stream. This happened when he and his eldest son, Musa Orwe stood on an ant hill and the animal aimed at him but his son, Musa Orwe narrowly escaped. This animal was later killed by the hunters. It was a sad moment that ignited the grief of many people from far and wide. He was mourned and eulogized as a hero.

Musa Orwe The Protagonist

Musa Auma Orwe was the firstborn son of Mathayo Orwe. He played a crucial role in initiating peace and uniting his siblings and step-mothers after his father's death. He extended this good gesture to Kanyotieno and even to Kanyikela community as a whole. He never liked conflict-ridden family quarrels and chaos. He would buy clothes and groceries to all his step-mothers. After graduating from Kamagambo Adventist College with a certificate in nursing, he started his first job at Gendia Mission hospital where he met his wife, Hawa Maira (Nyar Chief). Hawa's father, Samwel Dola, was the Chief of Karachuonyo. As a breadwinner in Kanyotieno family, Musa Orwe accommodated his siblings in his house at Gendia. He did this not only to his immediate members of family but also to friends and relatives who were eager to be educated. He took them to different technical schools and colleges where they could be trained to acquire different skills that would make them work to earn a living. Thanks to his wife, Hawa Maira who had a big heart to welcome all these people in her house. The friends and relatives who were accommodated in this house included people such as:

Isaya Okeno, Naum Ochieng, Roda Auma, Salome Awiti, Rufu Orwe (daughter to James Orwe), Joseph Odero Achola, Elkana Omolo (son of Sibia Omolo), Hulda Otieno, Elisaphan Akumu, Mahalone Ojwang Lwambe, Elijah Orwe and many others.

Musa Orwe was a team player of Kanyikela football Club where he was a super goalkeeper. During his school days at Rapedhi School, he resided at the home of Isaya Obiero where he became very close friend with Silfano Achola and Benjamin Anguk who were also football players. He was excited about development projects like education, agriculture, livestock keeping and business. The government officials from different places such as the Paul Mboya family of Karachuonyo liked his development initiatives and would pay him a visit from time to time to benchmark his ideas. This gesture almost ignited friction between him and some people who thought that he wanted to takeover the leadership of the Chief of West Nyokal Location which included the communities of Kwabwai, Kanyadoto and Kanyikela.

Musa Orwe died in 1953 when he was on a surgical operation at Gendia Mission Hospital where he was working. His death was a shock to many people. His funeral was attended by people of all races: The whites, Asians and Africans from different parts of the world who knew him and loved him. Many Children were named after him and that is why Musa Orwe is a household name in Kanyotieno family, Kanyikela community and Luo Nyanza in Kenya. Our gratitude goes to members of the Nyotieno family who have now emulated Musa Orwe and pushed his development agenda in areas such as education, agriculture, livestock keeping, business, church ministries, and other entrepreneurial activities.

The Orwe and Lwambe's Family Lineage

The Lwambe's Household

Since Elijah Lwambe was a staunch CMS Christian and evangelist, he had only one wife, Rael Ndiawo (Nyowino) from Nyakach Kadianga.

Joka Nyowino

Nyowino had two sons and three daughters. The sons were Isaya Okeno Lwambe and Mahalone Ojwang Lwambe and the daughters were Hanah Oluga (Min Ogare), who was married in Kanyada Kothidha by Wilson Obambo Ogare, Leah Adhiambo (Min Tom Onono), who was married in Gem Koguta Atieli by Haggai Onono and Elseba Aoko Odiembo (Min Atieno) who was married in Kanyadoto by Joshua Odiembo Agawo.

Joka Isaya Okeno

Isaya Okeno had three wives. The first one was Akeyo, daughter of Oloo (Akeyo Nyoloo). Akeyo Nyoloo had one daughter called Rusalia Lwambe (Min Olanda), named after Rusalia Nyapara, mother of Elijah Orwe. The second one was Christabel Oguta (Nyomoro). Oguta Nyomoro had a son called Charles Lwambe Okeno. The third one was Isdorah Akuku daughter of Oguna (Nyoguna). Nyoguna had four daughters and three sons. The daughters were: Mary Adhiambo, Jane Anyango (Mayor), Consolata Akinyi and Maren Atieno. The sons were: Peter Lwambe (Petro or Ombilo), John Okeno and Dancun Oginga Isaya. Isaya Okeno also married Willy Nyochieng (Bade Dongo) and Aduwo Nyar Kanyada. Both Willy Nyochieng and Aduwo nyar Kanyada did not have children.

Joka Mahalone Ojwang Lwambe

Mahalone Ojwang Lwambe had three wives: Marshela Anyango Ojwang, daughter of Elkana Mosi from Karachuonyo Konyango (Gendia), Matabel Arua Ojwang, daughter of Kitagre from Nyakach

Koguta (Pala) and Jane Aludo Ojwang, daughter of Aber Onyango from Kanyamwa. He also inherited Margaret Were, mother to Isack Ojwang and Grace Odoyo, mother to Maurice Ojwang. Margaret Were and Jane Aludo were sisters.

Joka Marshela Anyango Ojwang, Nyar Mosi (Min Apele)

Min Apele had nine sons: Eliud Otieno Ojwang, Wilbert Ojwang, Jack Francis Ojwang (Mowar), Moses Odera Ojwang, Ted Ojwang, Ezekiel Ogola Ojwang, Dr. Cainan Aol Ojwang, Shem Odoyo Ojwang, Omolo Agar Ojwang and three daughters: Damaris Aoko Ouko, Apeles Auma Ouko and Pamela Atieno Okundi.

Joka Matabel Arua Ojwang (Nyar Kitagre)

Matabel Arua Ojwang had three sons: Elly Ochieng Ojwang, Elijah Lwambe Ojwang, Joseph Odhiambo Ojwang and six daughters: Joyce Weke Ojwang, Nerea Auma Ojwang, Rose Akinyi Ojwang, Mary Akoth Ojwang, Millicent Adoyo Ojwang and Rosa Ojwang, named after Rosa Boyi Nyomogi (Mother of Pastor Sila Onyango).

Joka Jane Aludo Ojwang

Jane Aludo Ojwang had seven sons: Francis Onyango Ojwang, Nickanor Agonda Ojwang, Barack Odero Ojwang, Philip Ouma Ojwang, Pastor Erick Odira Ojwang, David Ojwang, Fred Ojwang and two daughters: Milcah Atieno Ojwang (Tieni) and Lillian Awuor Ojwang.

HISTORICAL FACTS ABOUT ELIJAH LWAMBE

Elijah Lwambe was a civil servant working for Railways company in Nairobi. He was converted to Church Missionary Society (CMS), the then Crown Church and became an evangelist of the CMS Church. His wife, Rael Ndiawo Nyowino gave birth to and raised two of her children, Hanah Oluga and Isaya Okeno in Nairobi. Both Elijah Lwambe and his wife, Rael Ndiawo (Nyowino) were very good at interpreting Kiswahili into the local Luo language.

MATHAYO ORWE'S HOUSEHOLD

Mathayo Orwe had three wives: Dina Achienge (Nyochuodho) from Kanyamwa, Rusalia Nyapara from Kabuoch Karading and Damar Aloo (Nyowiti) from Kanyamwa Kologi.

Joka Dina Achienge (Nyochuodho).

Dina Achienge had four sons and two daughters.

The daughters were: Ruth Oluga Akama (Married in Kabuoch Karading Obera), and Eunike Oreso Ndeda, married in Kanyadoto Karakor by Elder Harison Ndeda Minyaho. The Sons were: Musa Orwe, Petro Omollo Orwe, Daniel Okech Orwe and Elisafan Akumu.

Joka Musa Orwe

Musa Orwe's wife was Hawa Maira Orwe (Nyar Chief). She had three sons: Charles Owiti Orwe, Moses Ogungo Orwe and Geoffrey Odhiambo Orwe and seven daughters: Mary Adhiambo Dieto, Flounce Weke Mboya, named after Flora Weke, mother of Mathayo Orwe and Elijah Lwambe, Grace Rufu Abuya, Herine Ogembo, Jane Owili, Beldine Owuor and Olivia Achola Ranguma, wife of the First Governor of Kisumu County in Kenya, Jack Ranguma.

Joka Daniel Okech

Daniel Okech had one wife, Rebecca Omulo (Nyaringa), who had two sons and six daughters. The two sons were: Miltone Obote Orwe and Domnick Joel Ochieng Orwe. The six daughters were: Anyango, Rachel Weke, Grace Odero Odindo, Judith Akeyo Onyango, Benta Aoko Ooro, named after Gudu's wife, Ooro Nyar Nyambok, Emily Atieno and Ruth Achieng, named after Dina's first daughter, Ruth Akama.

Joka Elisafan Akumu

Elisafan Akumu was born after the death of Mathayo Orwe.

He had three wives: Dorina Arwa, Grace Abuya (Nyar Aron) and Benta Nyar Kowino Kagan. Nyar kowino never had children.

Joka Dorina Arwa

Dorina Arwa had four sons and three daughters:

The sons were: Samson Gudu, James Orwe, Benette Odhiambo (Atiaya) and Dennis Oliso. The daughters were: Agnes Auma, Mereza Anna Odero and Dinah Achieng.

Joka Grace Abuya (Nyar Aron).

Grace Abuya had two sons: Samson Ochieng (Winyo), Omondi Oliso and two daughters: Lucy Auma (Aluso), married in Kamgudho and Caroline Orwe (Mombasa).

Joka Rusalia Nyapara

Rusalia Nyapara was Mathayo Orwe's second wife after Dina Achienge. She had one son, Elijah Orwe and two daughters: Naum Ochieng Ogum (Min Ougo), who was married in Karachuonyo by Daniel Ogum and Ulda Otieno, married by Ratil Okoth from Kamenya.

Joka Elijah Orwe

Elijah Orwe had two wives, Lewnida Odete and Doris Adogo.

Joka Lewnida Odete (Min Musa)

Lewnida Odete had five sons and two daughters. The sons were: George Orwe, Antipas Omolo Orwe, Moses Ouma Orwe, Maira Orwe and Wycliffe Odiwuor Orwe. The Daughters were: Margaret Akinyi Orwe and Miriam Aoko Orwe.

Joka Doris Adogo (Min Alilo)

Doris Adogo had four sons and five daughters. The sons were: Lameck Ochieng Orwe, Wieland Ajuma Orwe, Omondi Orwe and Cliff Orwe (Soldier). The daughters were: Jane Orwe, Alilo Orwe, Anna Odero, Vida Atieno Orwe and Edna Orwe.

Joka Damar Aloo (Nyowiti)

Damar Aloo had two sons, Mudkayo Omollo and Joram Okola. She also had four daughters: Salome Awiti Nyabola, married to Musa Nyabola from Kasipul Kabondo, Rodah Auma, married to Zedekiah Akoth from Kamenya, Esta Anyango, married to Jekonia Omindi from Kanyamkago and Hellen Obuya, married to Hezekiah Oyugi from Imbo, Pe-Hill Akoko.

Joka Mudkayo Omolo

Mudkayo Omollo had five wives: Jenifa Auma (Nyar Owaga), Agness Kanini (Nyar Akamba), Rossy (Nyar Okech Owano), Jane Anyango (Nyar kamgudho) and Judith Akinyi (Nyar Gwasi). Nyar Kamgudho did not have children.

Joka Jenifa Auma (Nyar Owaga).

Auma Nyar Owaga had three sons: Musa Orwe Amudo, Samwel Owaga Amudo and Elly Wasonga Amudo.

Joka Kanini (Nyar Akamba)

Kanini Nyar Akamba had three sons and three daughters. The sons were: Silas Ochieng Amudo (Futo), Alphonce Omondi Amudo (Babu) and Victor Omolo Amudo. The daughters were: Mikal Mueni, Anastasia Akinyi and Damar Aloo, named after Damar Aloo (Nyowiti).

Joka Rossy Nyar Okech Owano

Nyar Okech Owano had a son called Agoyo wuon Otoke, named after Eliazar Agoyo, father to former Okebe of Kanyikela, Elkana Agola Agoyo.

Joka Judith Akinyi (Nyar Gwasi)

Nyar Gwasi had one son called Reuben Odongo and two daughters namely, Renalda Atieno and Diana Aoko.

Joka Joram Okola

Joram Okola had three wives: Susan Atieno Okola (Nyar Kamagambo), Filgona Atieno Okola (Nyar Kisumo) and Sabina Atieno Okola (Nyar Gwasi).

Joka Susan Atieno Okola (Min Paul)

Susan Atieno Okola had four sons and three daughters. The sons were: Paul Obiero Okola, Elphas Ochieng Okola, Moses Omondi Okola and Erick Okoth Okola. The daughters were: Millicent Awuor, Jackline Aoko and Lillian akinyi.

Joka Filgona Atieno Okola (Min Oloo).

Filgona Atieno Okola had four sons and two daughters. The sons were: Oloo Okola, Jared Okola, Tony Okola and Otish Okola. The daughters were: Banice Akoth and Molline Achieng.

Joka Sabina Atieno Okola (Min Dick)

Sabina Okola had five sons and one daughter. The sons were: Dickson Dulo Okola, Marcel Odiwuor Okola, Timothy Onyango Okola, Shem Odhiambo Okola (Elisha) and Walter Kasera Okola. She also had a daughter called Veronica Aloo, named after Damar Aloo (Nyowiti).

Historical Facts About Ka Orwe

Dina Achienge, Orwe's first wife was married in 1911. She died in 1981 at 88 years. Her first born son, Musa Orwe, was born in 1914. Musa Orwe wedded his wife, Hawa Maira in 1940. Hawa was born in 1921 and died in 2014. Musa Orwe died in 1953. Orwe's third born son, Elisafan Akumu died in 1992. He was a driver at Sony Sugar Company. Orwe's second born, Daniel Okech died in 1994. Daniel was born in 1927. Petro Omollo Orwe never married.

Kanyikela Pre-And Post Colonial Administrative System

Like all other communities, while in Central Nyanza-Asembo, Kanyikela had their administrative set up under family and Clan Traditional Leadership. They were later transformed into Local Native Legislative Council (LNLC) system for ease of administration. The Europeans only came to remodel and modernize them as they wanted. The indigenous people were choosing those to lead them including Legislative Council, the name of Parliament in the colonial era. Oyaya, father of Mathayo Orwe and Elijah Lwambe was one such leaders in Asembo, Central Nyanza. This Chiefdom system gave preferential treatment to some communities when people migrated and settled in South Kavirondo.

Gor Mahia The Paramount Traditional Chief of South Kavirondo

During the Pre-colonial period (1902-1904) the Traditional Chief was Gor Ogada (Gor Mahia). His mandates included: Right to allocate lands and right and authority to settle and re-settle communities. Gor settled Kanyikela people in Rangeya and Unga areas. These areas fell under Kanyikela Sub-Location in West Nyokal Location upto

1966. When appoinments were being made in West Nyokal Location Administrative Committees, Kanyikela Sub-Location used to have representatives from Rangenya and Unga areas. The first Kanyikela woman Paramount Elder, Bilia Onyango, mother of Prof. Jonathan Obel Onyango was from here alongside other Elders including Shem Barack Odero and Silfano Achola who represented Kanyikela in West Nyokal Local Native Legislative Council (LNLC.) The West Nyokal Locational Office was by then situated at Kobama. After the death of Gor Mahia, the paramount chief, the Kanyikela population in Rangenya and Unga areas were transmuted to East Konyango Location from West Nyokal Location. This was an act of "Divide and rule" as the scattered settlement ended up putting Kanyikela in the position of a minority population on both sides. This tyranny of numbers made Kanyikela for a long time to be traumatized and they always negatively suffered during personnel recruitments in public administrative offices. The following is the list of the West Nyokal administrators at that time. Most of them were either from Kanyadoto or Kwabwai communities because of their tyranny of numbers. None of them was from Kanyikela community. The administrators started as Traditional Elders and their tittles changed to Chiefs in the later years. In descending chronological order, they were: Ouko Obong from Kayadoto, Pundo Agola from Kanyadoto, Ondiek Ayieta from Kwabwai, Ogalo Opanga from Kanyadoto, Okita Agenga from Kanyadoto and Julius Ochieng Mita from Kanyadoto. This administrative scenario only changed in 1990 when Kanyikela was separated from Kanyadoto to have their own Location. Kanyikela Community is still not happy with the scenario where their companions in Rangenya are put in Kanyamwa Lower Kayambo Sub-Location and the residents therein including the Assistant Chief, Mr. Joseph Ambasa are all natives of Kanyikela. The Kanyikela Community genetic brothers in Unga are also under Unga Sub-Location, Kanyamwa East Location and the Assistant Chief, Mr. Nick Magambo is a grandson of the former Kobama Local Native Legislative Council (LNLC) representative of Kanyikela prior to 1966, the late Silfano Achola Athee.

Kanyadoto East Location
"Kanyikela Location"

On 7th February1990 the DO of Ndhiwa Mr. Daniel Masis went to Nguku Chief's Camp and declared Kanyikela a full Location under East Kanyadoto name. Kanyadoto Community was not pleased with this declaration and they hurled war threats. On 6th April 1990, The Homa-Bay DC Mr. William Kerario went to listen to the reasons why Kanyadoto did not want Kanyikela to be give a Location. On 11th April 1990 it was advertised on the Ndhiwa DO's notice board of a vacancy in East Kanyadoto Location and only inhabitants of Kanyikela were to apply for the position of the Chief. Twenty-four (24) natives of Kanyikela applied and nineteen (19) of them were shortlisted for an interview. As this process was on going, Kanyadoto Community put it on standard newspaper disputing this Kanyikela sovereignty. They also circulated war threat leaflets over Kanyikela independence. On 5th May 1990 another Homa-Bay DC Mr. Cyrus Gituai came for yet another conflict and dispute management but Kanyadoto still remained adamant. Despite all these threats, on 10th October1990 which was Moi Day, a national holiday, the Ndhiwa DO Mr. Daniel Masis announced it publicly at the Ndhiwa market arena that Kanyikela now have their own Location and he announced the name of the first Kanyikela Chief to be Mr. Francis Jack Ojwang (Mowar). The Location remained East Kanyadoto while it was made up of only Kanyikela natives. The genealogy of Francis Jack Ojwang, the First Chief of Kanyikela Location can be traced from top-down chronological order as from Ramogi to Kanyikela to Kowuor to ka Okal to Ka Nyamudho to Ka Odwo to Ka Lwambe to Ka Wagany to Ka Nyotieno to Ka Nyowino to Ka Mahalone Ojwang to Ka Nyar Mosi (Min Apele) to the nuclear family of Ka Jack Francis Ojwang (Mowar).

Previous Kanyikela Traditional Administrative Headmen Later Known as Assistant Chiefs

The following Kanyikela leaders exercised their administrative duties between 1904 to 2015. From the first to the last chronological order, they were:

1904-1913 - Andaro Odhiambo, ruled for nine (9) years.

1913-1927 - Akech Adongo, ruled for fourteen (14) years.

1928-1933 - Ochola Oucho, ruled for five (5) years.

1933-1934 - Gabriel Ogot, ruled for one (1) year.

1934-1943 - Nehemiah Ogutu, ruled for nine (9) years.

1944-1945 - Micah Awino, ruled for one (1) year.

1945-1951 - Yewa Okongo, ruled for six (6) years.

1951-1954 - Wilson Ododa Oyaya, ruled for three (3) years.

1954-1956 - Odhiambo Ododo, ruled for two (2) years.

1956-1973 - Eliakim Kasera, ruled for seventeen (17) years.

1973-1988 - Peter Elkana Agola, ruled for fifteen (15) years.

1988-2015 - Meshack Owino Okumu, ruled for twenty-seven (27) years. Meshack Owino Okumu also served as the Chief of South Kanyikela Location.

Historical Facts About Kanyikela Administration

John Ober elevated himself in the Kanyikela administration as the headman. He acted in this capacity for a period of six months. He was a trained nurse working in Kanyamkago area. He was later forced to hand over the leadership to Joshiah Obor who was also removed from the office due to integrity issues. There was an allegation against him that he misused his administrative powers to collect taxes from the Kanyikela Community for his personal gains.

Tracing Kanyotieno family from Kanyikela Community

LWAMBE HAD 3 WIVES:

1. Atweng'a-mother to Okuon.
2. Akal-mother to Asigo, Ogidi and Onyango.
3. Chicho- mother to Wagany.

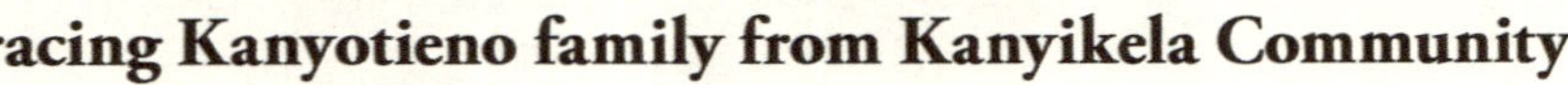

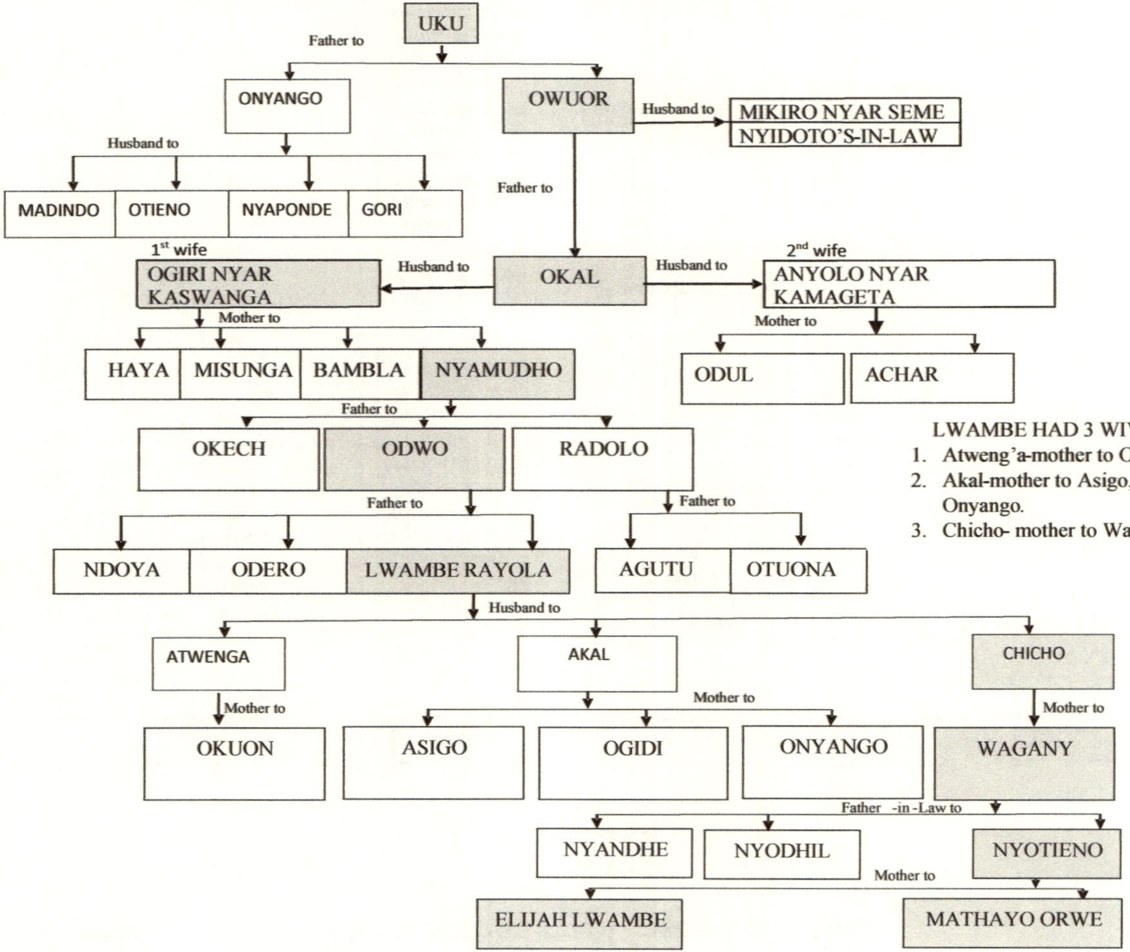

The descendants of Lwambe Rayola

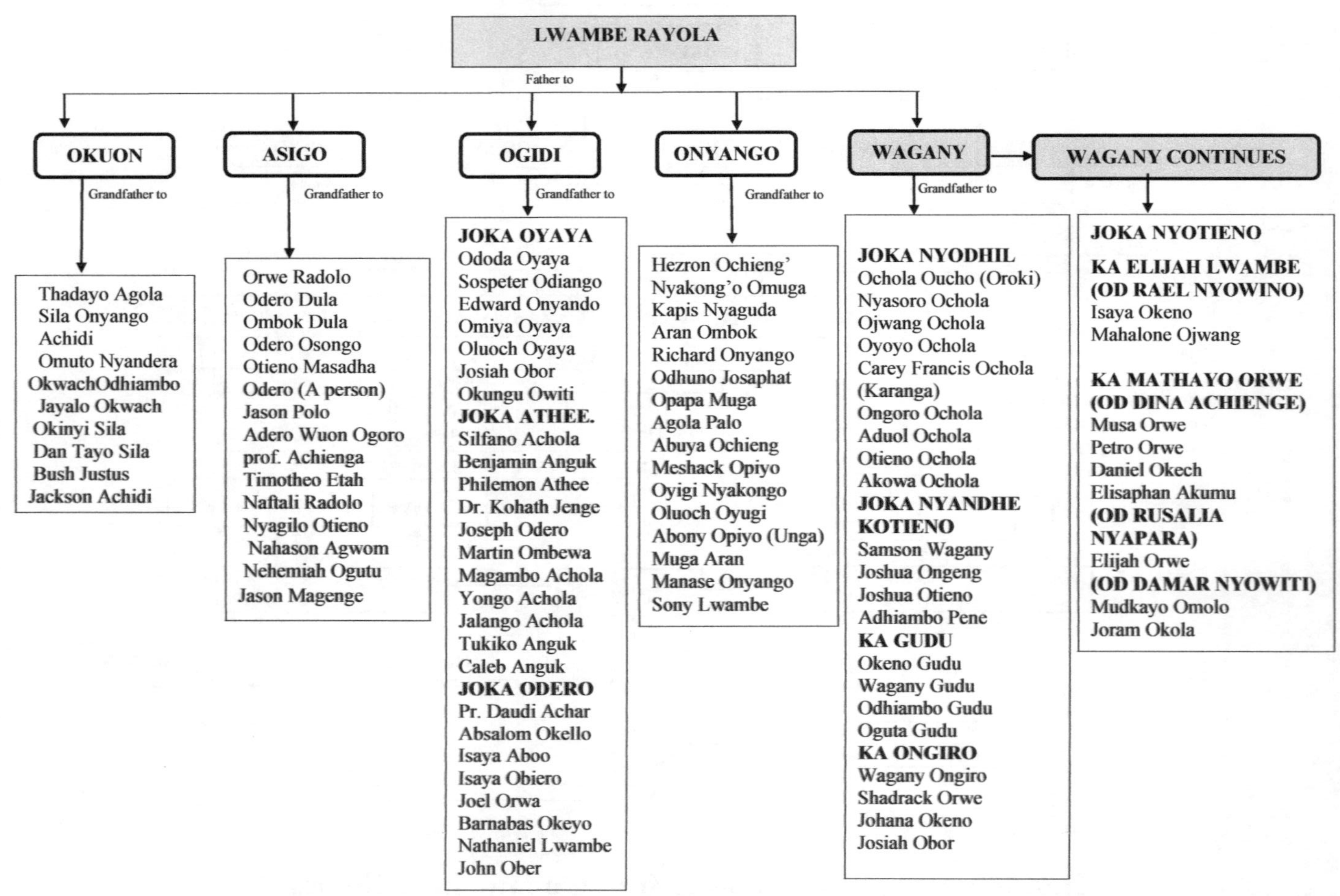

The Kawagany family

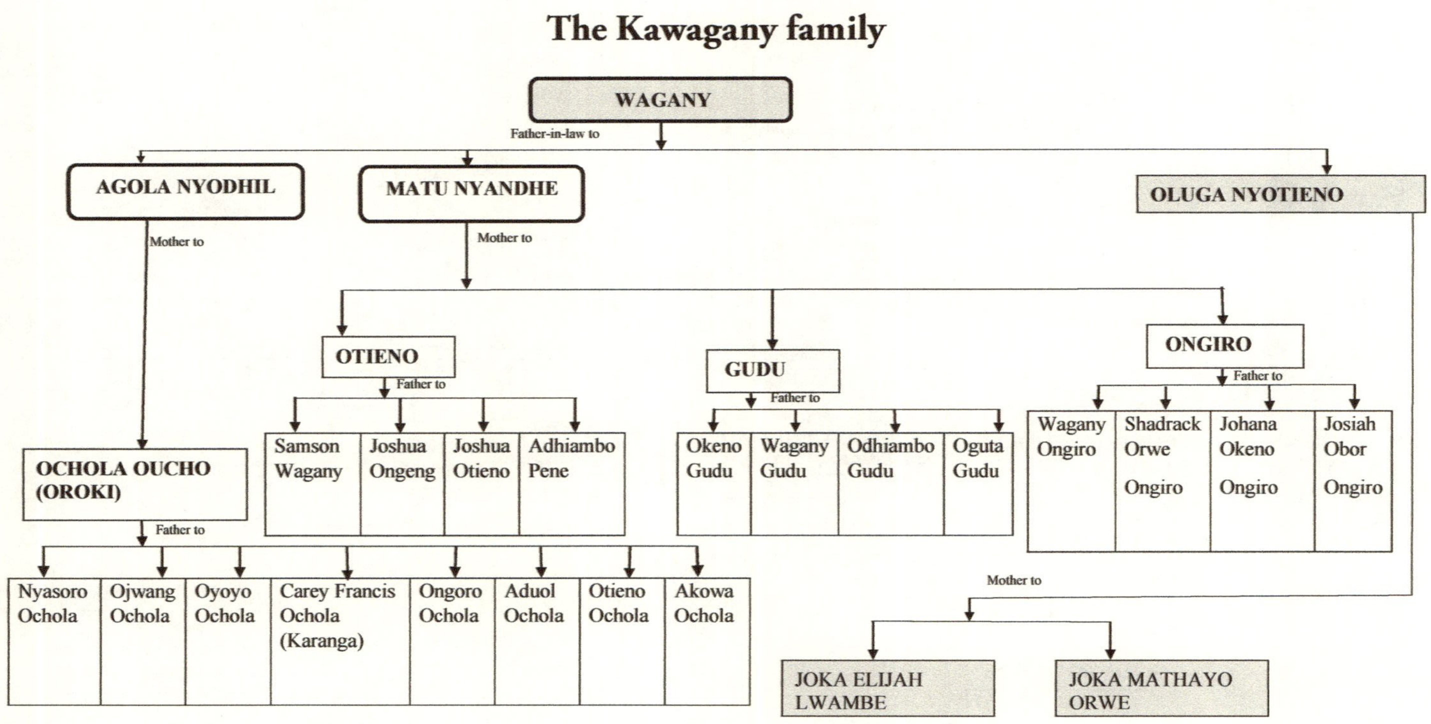

The Oluga Nyotieno family

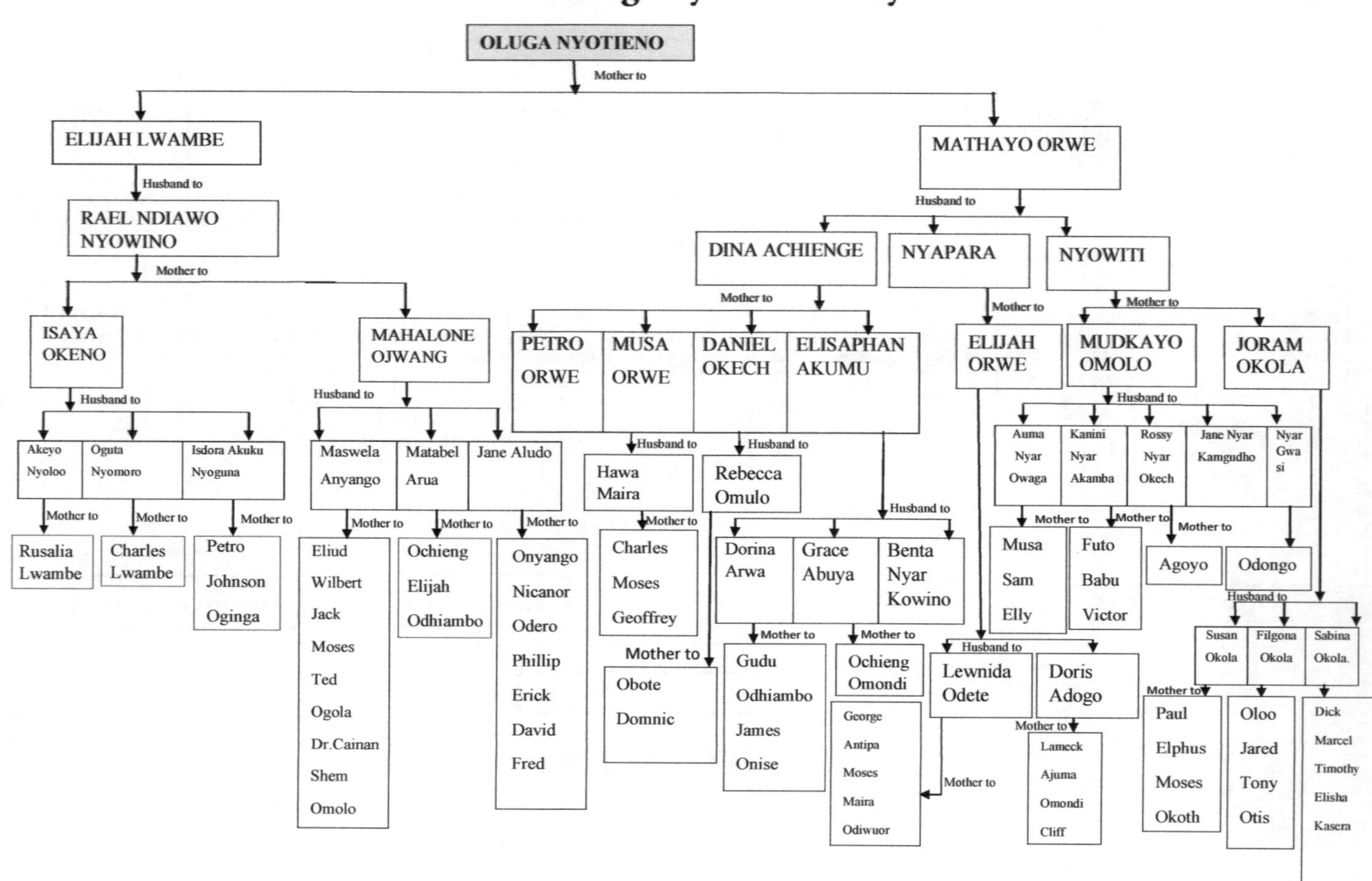

KANYOTIENO FAMILY PICTORIALS

Graduation at Maseno University in 2017.

From L to R: Janet Ojwang, Inan Ojwang,Dr. Cainan Ojwang,Dammary Ojwang, Sonia and Edwinner Ongati.

From L to R: Dr. Cainan Ojwang,Janet Ongati Ojwang and Dammary Wendy Ojwang.

Dr. Cainan Ojwang having a dance with his daughter, Dama.

Kanyotieno meeting at Nguku in 2015.

From L to R: The First Governor of Kisumu Hon. Jack Ranguma,Kenya-Re Camp meeting Pastor,Dr. Cainan Ojwang and The First Lady of Kisumu County, Hon.Olivia Ranguma.

From L to R: Dr. Cainan Ojwang,Rael Otieno(Dani),Evance Oyieke,Dady Manoah,Vincent Okundi,Job Odera, Mike Okoko, Minta and Madam Grace Ojwang at Kisumu in 2016.

Kanyotieno family meeting at Otange in 2016.

Min Apele,Mwalimu Eliud,Chief Jack Mowar,Mary Otieno(Mama Dani),Elly Ochieng, Nyar Kodongo,Min Nyagingo,Nyar suba and Kanyotieno children.

Madam Grace Ojwang,Janet Ongati Ojwang, Caren Obisa,Dr. Cainan Ojwang, Jack Francis Ojwang,Sonia and Inan Ojwang.

H.E. The First Governor of Kisumu Hon. Jack Ranguma,The First Lady Of Kisumu Hon.Olivia Ranguma,Madam Caroline Mwajuma,Pastor Dan Ongeto and Mr. John Otieno(Opecha) at Mowar's funeral in 2021.

Dr. Cainan Ojwang,Dana and Inan Ojwang.

Min Apele,Min Onyango and Min Aiso see us off to Subaland.

From L to R: Lameck Mowar (Otish),Jane Odera,Apeles Ouko,Sarah Okoko,Pamela Okundi,Dr. Cainan Ojwang and Manoah Mowar at Nguku in 2021.

From L to R: Dr. Cainan Ojwang,Jack Francis Ojwang,
Joseph Odhiambo Ojwang, Johnson Okeno and Elly
Ochieng at the high table in Subaland.

From L to R: Inan Ojwang,Janet Ojwang,Dammary
Ojwang and Dr. Cainan Ojwang in 2016.

From L to R: Joseph Osewe,Thomas Menya,Ezekiel Ogola,Enoch Ochieng Odiambo,Sam Odhiambo and Dama at
Lawrenceville,Georgia in 2021.

Mama Marshela Anyango Ojwang(min
Apele),Mary Otieno(Min Dani)Minta and
Sam Otieno at Homa-Bay in 1992.

Mwalimu Joram Lwambe Okola and Mzee Mahalone
Ojwang Lwambe.

Joram Okola and Elisaphan Akumu in 1964.

Mwalimu Joram Okola among the Luo Council of
Elders at Hon. Raila Odinga's home.

Joram Okola among the Luo Council of Elders at Raila Odinga's home.

Dani Damar Aloo Orwe.

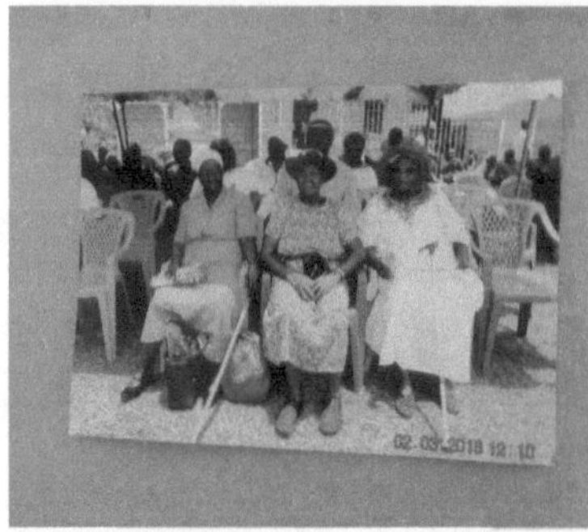

Mama Marshela Anyango Ojwang(Min Apele),Waya Naum Ogum and Waya Hellen Obuya in 2018.

Mzee Elijah Orwe, Mwalimu Erick Ochieng Odiembo and some visitors at Rapedhi in early 1970s.

Patron of Kanyotieno family, Joram Okola with Ndhiwa Administration Officers.

Waya Leah Adhiambo Onono,Mama Lewnida Odete Orwe and Waya Hanah Oluga Obambo.

Kanyotieno family Patron,Joram Lwambe Okola among the Luo Council of Elders at Hon. Raila Odinga's home.

Peter Lwambe(Ombilo) and some members of the Nyotieno family at a funeral in 2018.

Prime Minister, Hon. Raila Odinga is welcomed by Joram Okola(Chairman-Ndhiwa Luo Council of Elders)during the official opening of Kisumu International Airport in 2012.

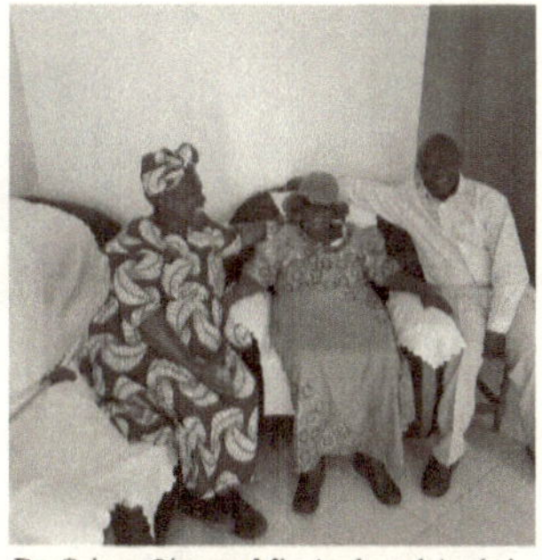

Dr. Cainan Ojwang, Min Apele and Apele in 2019.

Mama Hawa Maira Orwe,Her daughters and grand daughters.

Mama Hawa Maira Orwe(Nyar Chief), her father, Chief Daniel Dola and her step mothers.

Standing L To R: Mama Doris Adogo Orwe,Mzee Nathaniel Lwambe and Mama Isdora Akuku Isaya(Nyoguna).
Sitting LtoR: Mama Loyce Lwambe(Min Odete), Marshela Anyango (Min Apele) Mzee Mahalone Ojwang, Mwalimu John Koko and Mwalimu Rebeca Koko.

Mzee Mahalone Ojwang with some of his children, Filiph Lwambe Ojwang, Fenstis Onyango Ojwang,Joseph Odhiambo Ojwang and Nicanor Agwede Ojwang Standing at the background is Maurah Ojwang (Daily Mower).

Waya Elseba Aoko Odiembo(Min Atieno) and Mzee Joshua Odiembo Agawo.

Mzee Joram Okola and Mama Isdora Akuku (Nyoguna).

Dr. Cainan Ojwang among Gendia High School students in 1985.

Mama Isdora Akuku (Nyoguna).

Mzee Isaya Okeno and Mama Isdora Akuku(Nyoguna).

Mzee Mahalone Ojwang and Mami Jane Airdo Ojwang

From Lto R: Dr. Cainan Ojwang,Moses Odere Ojwang,Madam Grace Ojwangwith her children Sam and Otieh in early 1980s.

Mama Matabel Arwa Ojwang (Nyar Kitagre)

Mzee Mahalone Ojwang and Mama Marshela Anyango Ojwang in Nairobi.

Ezekiel Ogola Ojwang and Tom Onono at Agoro Sare High School in 1979.

Mzee Musa Orwe and Mama Hawa Maira Orwe in early 1950s.

Bob Ochieng's uncle making a point at Jack Mowar's funeral. Mr. Milton Obote serves as the master of ceremony while Mwalimu Eliud Otieno listens carefully.

From LtoR: Apeles Ouko, Pamela Okundi, Dr. Cainan Ojwang, Ezekiel Ogola and Eliud Otieno.

Dr. Cainan Ojwang, Inan Ojwang and their visitor in Kisumu, Kenya.

From LtoR: Apeles Ouko, Mary Oyieke(Nyar Waya Hana Obambo) and Pamela Okundi

From L to R: Mama Doris Adogo Orwe, Mama Anna Nyowaga, Mama Susan Atieno Okola, Mzee Joratn Okola Mama Lewnida Orwe, Mama Sabina Okola and Mama Filgona Okola.

Ezekiel Ogola Ojwang making a point at Chief Francis Jack Ojwang's funeral in 2021.

Chief Francis Jack Ojwang's daughters-in-law and some of his sons.

From Lto R: Sam Mowar,Dody Mowar,Dady Mowar,Apeles Ouko,Madam Grace Ojwang, Ezekiel Ogola and Dr. Cainan Ojwang.

Francis Jack Ojwang's grand children.

From LtoR: Jim Ochieng Menya and his family,David Odera,Apeles Ouko,Minta,Brian Onyango and Nyar Suba at Mowar's burial site.

From LtoR: Grace Odoyo,Roseline Otieno(Nyar Kobiero),Jane Odera,Madam Grace Ojwang(Min Otish),Caroline Mwajuma and Dr.Jane Obura.

From Lto R: Dady Mowar,Apeles Ouko, Pamela Okundi, Dr. Cainan Ojwang,Jane Odera,Eliud Otieno,Elly Ochieng,Rose Akinyi,Marytrizer Osee and Mary Akoth.

From Lto R: Apeles Ouko,Pamela Okundi,Jane Odera,Eliud Otieno and Dr. Cainan Ojwang.

From Lto R:Otis Mowar,Joseph Odhiambo Ojwang,Mrs. Dady Mowar,Mrs. Sam Mowar,Mrs. Mike Mowar,Dady Mowar,Apeles Ouko,Pamela Okundi Dr. Cainan Ojwang and Eliud Otieno.

From LtoR: The first Governor of Kisumu Hon. Jack Ranguma, Joffrey Orwe, Jack Ojwang(Mowar),Apeles Ouko and John Ouko.